SEMINAR STUDIES IN HISTORY

Editor: Patrick Richardson

James I

SEMINAR STUDIES IN HISTORY

Editor: Patrick Richardson

A full list of titles in this
series will be found on the
back cover of this book

SEMINAR STUDIES IN HISTORY

James I

S. J. Houston

LONGMAN

LONGMAN GROUP LIMITED
London

*Associated companies, branches and
representatives throughout the world*

First Published 1973
Second Impression 1975

ISBN 0 582 35208 8

Printed in Great Britain by
Lowe & Brydone (Printers) Ltd, Thetford, Norfolk

Contents

Part One · Background

Part Two · Analysis

Part Three · Assessment

Part Four · Documents 111

Introduction to the Series

The seminar method of teaching is being used increasingly. It is a way of learning in smaller groups through discussion, designed both to get away from and to supplement the basic lecture techniques. To be successful, the members of a seminar must be informed – or else, in the unkind phrase of a cynic – it can be a 'pooling of ignorance'. The chapter in the textbook of English or European history by its nature cannot provide material in this depth, but at the same time the full academic work may be too long and perhaps too advanced.

For this reason we have invited practising teachers to contribute short studies on specialised aspects of British and European history with these special needs in mind. For this series the authors have been asked to provide, in addition to their basic analysis, a full selection of documentary material of all kinds and an up-to-date and comprehensive bibliography. Both these sections are referred to in the text, but it is hoped that they will prove to be valuable teaching and learning aids in themselves.

Note on the System of References:

A bold number in round brackets (5) in the text refers the reader to the corresponding entry in the Bibliography section at the end of the book.

A bold number in square brackets, preceded by 'doc' [docs 6, 8] refers the reader to the corresponding items in the section of Documents, which follows the main text.

PATRICK RICHARDSON
General Editor

Acknowledgements

My thanks are due to three friends who have helped in the preparation of this book. Anthony Davidson and Michael Wood gave generously of their time in reading and commenting on the text. Patrick McGrath, whose mellow teaching first stimulated my interest in James I, gave me much valuable advice and encouragement, and saved me from error. It is to him that this book is affectionately dedicated.

S.J.H.
Bristol Grammar School, 1972

We are grateful to the following for permission to reproduce copyright material:

The American Philosophical Society for an extract from *The Letters of John Chamberlain*, edited by N. E. McClure, *Memoirs of the American Philosophical Society*, Vol. 12, 1939; The Trustees of the British Museum for extracts from the *Harleian Manuscripts*, fols. 196/7 and 202; Jonathan Cape Ltd, for an extract from *James VI and I* by D. H. Wilson, quoted from the Salisbury Manuscript III, 59/61 and Edward M. Wilson for an extract from the translation of the letter from Don Carlos Coloma to the Count-Duke of Olivares.

The photograph on the cover is the James I medal commemorating peace with Spain 1604 and is reproduced by courtesy of the Trustees of the British Museum.

PART ONE

Background

1 James VI & I

Queen Elizabeth I died at Richmond between two and three o'clock in the morning of 24 March 1603, her crown and titles passing without incident to her cousin James VI of Scotland. For years the Queen's chief minister, Robert Cecil, and other important Englishmen had been secretly in touch with James to ensure their future and to make sure that nothing impeded the accession of this great-grandson of Henry VIII's sister Margaret. From York the Lord President of the Council of the North wrote to Cecil saying: 'The contentment of the people is unspeakable, seeing all things proceed so quietly, whereas they expected in the interim their houses should have been spoiled and sacked.' By the 1620s the English would feel nostalgic about 'good Queen Bess', but now they were glad to have done with petticoat government and relieved that the succession was undisputed (97).

Those who rushed to see James as he made his leisurely progress south were not unimpressed by what they saw. Modern writers, repeating the spiteful reminiscences of Sir Anthony Weldon, are inclined to emphasise the undignified aspects of the king and to find them unedifying [doc. 2]. Contemporaries did not see it this way. James in his middle age was no more grotesque than Elizabeth in hers: to most of their subjects they were both majestic. James was thirty-seven when he came into his kingdom but looked slightly younger. In person he was of medium height. He had pale blue eyes, eloquent of wariness and humour, a broad brow and a full head of brown hair. He wore a thin, square-cut beard. An illusion of corpulence was much enhanced by the wearing of a quilted doublet for protection from the daggers of assassins — probably unnecessary in England but a wise precaution in Scotland. In dress he was conventional, old-fashioned, untidy; in old age he became slovenly. Throughout his later years he was troubled, and sometimes incapacitated by porphyria, accompanied by what his physician described as 'terrifying insomnia, turbulent nights, laboured breathing, palpitation' and the appearance of 'frank delirium with hallucinations' (103).

His melancholies were brief and quickly relieved so that most of the court regarded him as quietly jovial. He was by nature sociable and hospitable, but took no pleasure in large gatherings. 'The access of the people made him so impatient that he often dispersed them with frowns, and on being told that they only wished to see his face, he cried out: "God's wounds! I will pull down my breeches and they shall also see my arse".' His plain speaking, always clear and often vulgar, was a refreshing change from Elizabeth's equivocations. He loved to argue. 'The Learned stood about him at his Board', wrote Hacket, a small group whose conversation ranged from the general to the ecclesiastical, where full attention would be given to the king's learning and bawdy jests [doc. 3]. He endeared himself easily to the young and to the families of his favourites, and enjoyed a series of intimate, and possibly homosexual associations with beautiful young men, to whom he would address mawkish verses and send rich presents. Most other of his acquaintances were subject to genial ridicule, like Cecil, who was called the 'little beagle that lies by the fire when all the good hounds are daily running in the fields'.

The king loved equally theology and the chase, disputing privately with his divines and publicly, in print, with Arminian and Catholic controversialists. He aspired to literary fame, translating the French poet Sallust du Bartas and the Psalms of David into English doggerel. As a writer of prose he was genuinely gifted. His political, controversial and religious writings reveal the penetrating intelligence that lay behind the homely exterior (10). He was shrewd, wily and persistent, having displayed at moments of crisis in Scotland a courage and patience that did him great credit. His reckless horsemanship, conspicuous even in a kingdom said to be paradise for women and hell for horses, contradicts the oft-repeated gossip of Sir John Oglander that 'James was the most cowardly man that ever I knew' (16).

He was more munificent than his means allowed, delighting to give. He never saved a shilling. He disliked work and wanted to make a quick end of it, much preferring to hunt than to study state papers. He disliked injustice and, in an intolerant age, was broadminded and tolerant. In the 1590s he had taken part in the famous Scottish witch trials, interrogating captives and asking them to play him the devil's tune to which they danced. In later years he was less credulous. He applied his sharp mind and common sense to the exposure of imposters, becoming increasingly sceptical of the activities of evil spirits.

Like most men, praise delighted him. Surrounded by fawning courtiers he received more flattery in England than was good for him. As Arthur Wilson observed: 'But our king coming through the North (Banqueting and Feasting by the way) the applause of the people in so obsequious and submissive a manner (still admiring change) was checked by an honest plain Scotsman (unused to hear such humble Acclamations) with a Prophetical expression: This people will spoil a good king' (24). As ruler of Scotland James had served a long, arduous and highly successful apprenticeship in the art of kingcraft. Separated from his mother, Mary Stuart, and crowned King of Scotland at the age of thirteen months, his rigorous education began almost before he had ceased to be a baby. Two tutors were appointed shortly after his third birthday: George Buchanan, an aged scholar of international repute, ill tempered and severe; and Peter Young, a gentle young man of twenty-seven, educated in Geneva under the guidance of his uncle Henry Scrimgeour, a great humanist, bibliophile and jurist. It would have been difficult to equal in Europe the pedagogical skills of this team. Buchanan insisted with ferocious intensity that 'a king ought to be the most learned clerk in his dominions', and James was forced to make the most of his very formidable intelligence. Instead of turning into the usual princely parody of the Renaissance ideal of the Whole Man – bad at everything – the king grew up with a deep understanding of history, theology and the classics, becoming an author of considerable distinction [doc. 1]. James was not, however, left to study in tranquillity. Throughout his childhood and adolescence he was the victim of factional plots which aimed at controlling the state by seizing his person. The psychological shock of these bloody affrays, called 'ruffles' by the Scots, was in no way cushioned by an affectionate home. James grew up alone, starved of the love, kindness and stability which usually come from a happy family life.

After attaining his majority in 1587 James set about asserting his independence, so that eventually he, and not Maitland, his chief minister, determined policy. As early as 1583 James had proclaimed his intention to 'draw his nobility to unity and concord and to be known as a universal king'. In a kingdom seething with baronial riot, royal government was challenged by two groups of extremists: the conservative lords of the North led by the Earl of Huntly, and the Ultra-Protestants led by the Earl of Bothwell. The Northern Earls are called the 'Catholic' faction, not for their religious zeal but for their political conservatism and hostility to Presbyterianism. Unwilling to recognise the significance of Spain's defeat when the Armada was wrecked, Huntly corresponded with Philip II and encouraged him to try again. For this, and for occasional acts of rebellion, he was imprisoned but always eventually pardoned. The king's leniency was criticised as indefensible favouritism. Yet it is hard to see what else he could have done, lacking as he did the physical resources for repressive measures. Without a standing army James could make his rule effective only by balancing the factions and discreetly using force when it was available. James needed Huntly — who was probably his closest friend at this time — as an ally against the terrifying Bothwell. By refusing to persecute Catholics James avoided the risk of assassination at the hand of a fanatic, and at the same time ensured his future should England be defeated by Spain.

The Ultra-Protestants were particularly resentful of James's reluctance to crush the Northern Earls. Since Mary's death, and the establishment in 1586 of the alliance with England, they had little pretext for action against the government. Their leader, Francis Stewart Hepburn, fifth Earl of Bothwell, was more interested in pursuing an ancestral feud against Maitland than in advancing the interests of Presbyterianism. Bothwell made trouble on the border, flouted royal authority and was supported by the ministers, one of whom described him as a sanctified plague sent by God to turn the king from evil. When, after being proclaimed an outlaw, he joined forces with the rebellious Catholic Earls, the Kirk turned against him. After this rebellion had failed he fled abroad and died in Naples.

Nothing better illustrates the king's political sagacity than his handling of the long battle with the Kirk. In December 1560 the Presbyterians had established the General Assembly of the Kirk of Scotland, comprising representatives of the nobility, the burghs and the clergy. Although its legal position was uncertain (a fact that James would later exploit) the Assembly drew up plans for the day-to-day running of the church. Three dioceses were governed by bishops who had joined the revolt against Mary. Five superintendents were appointed by the state to watch over ecclesiastical affairs in the regions, and a few commissioners, appointed by the Assembly, undertook similar responsibilities in the remaining areas. The vexed question of whether or not to retain episcopacy erupted in 1571, when the government appointed ministers to be archbishops of Glasgow and St Andrews. The General Assembly reluctantly agreed, but insisted that the government's nominees must be approved by a committee of ministers and be subject to the Assembly. This far from satisfactory settlement was undermined by Andrew Melville (1545-1622), a distinguished scholar who returned from Geneva in 1574 to become principal of Glasgow University. Melville advocated a strict Presbyterianism. The church should be governed not by bishops or superintendents but by committees (presbyteries) of ministers. All ministers were equal, a principle not to be violated by the tyranny of episcopacy. The Kirk, he declared, possessed an authority which, derived from God, was superior to the authority of the state. He told James that there were two kings in

Scotland, one of whom was Christ Jesus, whose kingdom was the Kirk, of which James was 'not a king, nor a lord, nor a head, but a member'. Supreme authority in the Kirk must rest with the General Assembly which, under Melville's influence, was remodelled to represent not the three estates but only the ministers and elders of the church. James, as a member of the Kirk, was expected to listen to advice from the pulpit on every aspect of his public and private life.

Although Melville's beliefs threatened royal authority, his strength was more apparent than real. Many of the Reformers were suspicious of his views and quite prepared to accept the episcopacy approved by the Crown. The second generation of Protestant nobility were less fervent than their fathers, while many of the laity resented the claims of the ministers. Moreover, from many points of view James was an ideal Protestant king, learned, patient and a patron of Presbyterian divines. So long as the Catholics were a danger at home and abroad James avoided a clash with the Kirk. He cleverly enticed the ecclesiastical opposition away from Bothwell without making any important concessions. Encroachments by the Presbyterians on episcopal authority were tactfully ignored. Then, in 1596, the extremist ministers overreached themselves providing James with an opportunity for action against them. Andrew Melville accused the General Assembly of treason against Christ for approving James's reconciliation with the rebellious Northern Earls. When, in September, he was granted his famous interview with James, Melville 'bore him down, calling the king but God's silly [weak] vassal'. James listened to the lecture with amazing patience and bided his time. The ministers continued to behave outrageously. They tried to prevent trade with Catholic France and Spain, and rebuked the queen for frivolity and the king for using intemperate language. David Black, minister of St Andrews, proclaimed from the pulpit his discovery that 'all kings are devils' children'. He denounced Elizabeth as an atheist, asserted that James intended to bring the full rigours of episcopacy to Scotland and, when hauled before the Council, refused to recognise its jurisdiction. In November the ministers demanded that king and Council should be called to account for 'their negligence in hearing the Word'. By the end of the year James sensed that the zealots were in danger of isolating themselves from the main body of ministers. He therefore ordered the commissioners of the Kirk to leave the capital, forbade speeches against the government and insisted that ministers accused of sedition should submit to the Council. When the ministers confected a popish scare, James, to mark his displeasure, moved himself, his household and the law courts to Linlithgow. Edinburgh wilted before the king's wrath, and the city fathers agreed not to admit any ministers without the king's consent. James now proceeded, by a series of ingenious manoeuvres, to tame the General Assembly. He asserted his right under an Act of 1592 to convene the Assembly when and where he pleased, so that it now met irregularly in the more conservative regions north of the Tay. Bereft of its leaders, the Assembly meekly passed measures which destroyed the political threat of Presbyterianism (34).

Once the power of the extremists was destroyed, James set about strengthening episcopacy as a way of checking the obnoxious doctrine of the parity of all ministers 'whereby the ignorant are emboldened to cry down their betters' (*Basilikon Doron*). Quietly and without offence he appointed new bishops to the sees of Aberdeen, Ross and Caithness. Gradually, during the early seventeenth century, the status and powers of the bishops were increased, so that they became influential agents of the royal will in both Church and State.

James VI's success in establishing his authority over the nobility and the Kirk should not obscure what was possibly his most enduring achievement: his success in bringing about a new respect for law and order. Duelling was forbidden. Parties to a feud were summoned before the Council and obliged to swear, under heavy penalties, to keep the peace. Nobles who kept large retinues, or who in any way challenged the Crown, were punished. Much was done to extend the benefits of royal government to the Border, the Highlands and the Western Isles. By the early seventeenth century, therefore, the king's passion for law and order had brought to Scotland an unaccustomed peace which, by encouraging trade, began to promote prosperity. His achievement 'in solving problems which had been outstanding for generations, can fairly be described as spectacular' (34, p. 234).

James's highly successful rule over Scotland justified his claim to be 'an experienced king needing no lessons'. His character was moulded in the North, where the various difficulties he encountered inevitably coloured his attitude towards many of the problems that faced him in England (86). His unfortunate childhood fathered a complex, neurotic adult. His love of peace, his aversion to forceful action of any kind, owed something to what he had suffered during his minority. The emphasis he placed on Divine Right was partly a response to Buchanan's political theories and Melville's doctrine of the two kingdoms, and partly a reaction against the lordly anarchy of the nobility. His experience of government taught him to be cautious, conciliatory and, when necessary, tough. He was prepared to gain his ends by dissimulation. Conflict with the Presbyterians left him with a lifelong distrust of Puritanism. Writing of this part of James's life, Professor

Donaldson has described the king as 'a man of very remarkable political ability and sagacity in deciding on policy and of conspicuous tenacity in having it executed. He may not have been the ablest of the Stewarts, but he was assuredly the most successful of his line in governing Scotland and bending it to his will' (**34**, p. 214).

In the light of this judgment, and the evidence on which it is based, it becomes difficult to explain the relative failures of James's later years. The problems he faced were greater, yet his response was less astute, probably because his judgment was deadened by flattery. James had always thought highly of himself, but in Scotland his conceit was regularly punctured by plain speaking and outright opposition from men close to the government. In the enervating atmosphere of the south he was surrounded by obsequious courtiers and encouraged to believe that he was invariably right. Moreover, he was no longer in his prime. A sixteenth-century writer compared the Stuart kings with horses from the district of Mar 'which in youth are good but in their old age bad'. By 1620, when a tangle of foreign and domestic problems required urgent attention, the king was fifty-four, an old man by Stuart standards, and stricken with illness. It is probable, too, that James, who had long waited and schemed for his inheritance, was determined to relax and enjoy it. His great work was done and he could now look forward to a happy retirement. Unaware of the cussedness of Elizabeth's later parliaments, of the growth of faction and corruption in government, accustomed to a subservient Scottish parliament where the gentry were of no account, he expected little opposition to his will. Years of penury in an economically backward country left him ill-equipped to face either the complexities of England's financial affairs or the harsh fact that the Crown's wealth was not prodigious. James therefore gave and spent magnificently, making less effort than before to assess the problems of his situation and to calculate the best possible remedies.

2 James's Inheritance

PEOPLE, WORK AND WEALTH

The English, during the early seventeenth century, were living through a period of inflation and population growth. Although there is uncertainty about the rate of growth, England's population had climbed from about 3 million in 1530 to over 4 million in 1603 (**43**). Between 1530 and 1640 the general price level rose five times, the price of wheat six times. If the causes of inflation are controversial, the effects are plain (**109**). As prices rose, wages lagged behind, encouraging the capitalist employer while depressing the living standards of most of the people. Those producing food for market prospered agreeably. Landlords living on fixed incomes had to adapt or decline. The monarch, whose revenues from land and feudal dues failed to match the rising costs of government, was compelled to search for new ways of raising money.

Although agriculture remained the basis of the economy, there occurred between 1540 and 1640 a remarkable expansion of trade and industry, which affected only a tiny proportion of the population. By 1640 the truth of John Cleveland's words, 'Correct your maps; Newcastle is Peru', was manifest, coal production having risen from 200,000 tons a year in 1540 to 1.5 million tons a century later. Iron production increased fivefold during the same period, while advances also occurred in the manufacture of soap, bricks and glass, and in the smelting of iron ore, the refining of salt and the brewing of beer (**74**). England's principal industry was the manufacture of woollen cloth, which represented three-quarters of her exports. The fine wool of England had traditionally been made up into broadcloths, the bulk of which was shipped, undyed, to the Continent. Broadcloth manufacture was declining by the end of the sixteenth century, and while retaining considerable importance, its place was being taken by the so-called New Draperies. These were cloths of the worsted type, lighter and frequently cheaper than the traditional broadcloths. The industry was subject to severe fluctuations. After a decade of prosperity the export trade declined after 1614 and the last five years of James's reign were cursed by a severe depression (**67**).

Although an overwhelming majority of people lived in the country, the upward surge of population and the growth of trade and industry led to an expansion of the towns. The growth of London was spectacular. To contemporaries it seemed grotesque, and they compared the realm to a man suffering from rickets, his head too big for his body. Inhabited by about 50,000 people in Henry VIII's time, the city had grown to contain perhaps a quarter of a million by 1603. It sucked up immigrants, manufactures and food in abundance. All attempts to regulate its growth failed and it became, especially in the parishes to the east of the old city walls, a jerry-built teeming slum (30). Outside the capital only a handful of towns, such as Bristol, York and Norwich housed more than 10,000 souls. Provincial seaports, like Hull, Bristol, Exeter, Lynn, Newcastle and Glasgow, collected from their hinterland the iron and manufactures, the cloth and agricultural produce, that formed the basis of their prosperity. A considerable part of their trade was with London where the great merchant companies tended to dominate foreign trade. By 1600, for instance, seven-eighths of the export trade in cloth was monopolised by London merchants. This helped to create a division of interest between those London merchants who played a major role in the monopolistic companies for foreign trade and the merchants of the outports, who wanted to whittle down the privileges of societies like the Merchant Adventurers or the East India Company.

Industry and commerce in Jacobean England were on a small scale. Agriculture remained the concern of perhaps four-fifths of the population. An increasing urban population had stimulated demand for food and clothing, so that there was every incentive to commercialise agriculture. A determined attempt was made, during the sixteenth and early seventeenth centuries, to transform fixed rents paid by tenant farmers into short-term leases, so that rents could be periodically raised. The enclosure of open fields and waste proceeded apace, either for sheep rearing or to facilitate agricultural improvements. It is probable that complaints during James's reign about the enclosure of arable were exaggerated. Most enclosure took place before 1603, and even then progress was slow. Those landlords who were willing to drain land, use fertilisers and rationalise the management of their estates enjoyed great prosperity.

Although the social structure of the period 1500-1640 has been widely discussed in recent years, historians have yet to unravel satisfactorily the intricate relationships that exist between politics and social change in seventeenth century England (66). The ruling class was a closely knit group of hereditary peers and landed gentry. Whether rising or declining, recent or ancient families, all were dependent on land for their position in society. The structure of this society was hierarchical, an 'inequality of states, orders and degrees appointed by God'. Status, not class, dominated contemporary social thinking. Thomas Wilson the antiquarian observed, in his *State of England Anno Dom. 1600*, that the uppermost status group was a twofold *nobilitas* consisting of the peerage and a lesser nobility of knights, esquires and gentlemen (**25**). The titled nobility were few but influential. They had once been the most important people in English life and politics, controlling the House of Commons, dominating the counties and meddling in royal administration. They had made and unmade kings. During the sixteenth and early seventeenth centuries they experienced a serious, though temporary slump in power and prestige. Professor Stone has tried to explain the reasons for this phenomenon (**65**). He has shown that by the end of the sixteenth century most of the peers were beginning to face the facts of economic life and, having great reserves to draw upon, recovered. If their political power and prestige declined, the rights and privileges of the peerage, their influence and social pre-eminence remained unimpaired. Socially and politically they were still very important in Jacobean England, though they probably had more influence individually in the counties than collectively in the House of Lords.

The privileges and responsibilities of the governing class were enjoyed by the gentry as well as the nobility. James Harrington, in his book *Oceana* (1656), assumed that the work of government was a thing 'peculiar unto the genius of a Gentleman'. The possession of freehold land to the value of forty shillings, together with the right to bear arms, was all that was needed for the acquisition of gentry status. Neither presented an insuperable barrier to a man with money. 'As for gentlemen, they be made good cheap in England', wrote Sir Thomas Smith in 1565.' 'For whosoever . . . can live idly and without manual labour, and will bear the part, charge and countenance of a gentleman . . . shall be taken for a gentleman.' The inflation and rising population of this period established conditions conducive to the prosperity of landlords, if they had the drive to take advantage of them. Landed incomes, especially from the late sixteenth century onwards, rose steeply (**64**). Those who failed to adjust to the new conditions stagnated or else declined (**66**). Those who mattered most were not the lesser gentry on the fringe of the ruling class, but the rich gentry who dominated the counties. It was they who provided three-quarters of the members of the House of Commons during James's reign, sitting for most of the borough as well as the county seats.

Although agriculture was the largest single source of wealth, vast fortunes were made by a small group of export merchants and financiers. Some of the great London merchants were as rich as peers and were drawn more and more into money-lending, principally to the Crown. Many were knighted by James and some became peers. They dominated the government of the City of London and were often members of parliament too. With their estates in the country, they had more in common with the ruling class than with other groups in society. The inferiority of the middle and lower degrees derived from their involvement in occupations lacking in honour. This is why many seventeenth-century writers denied that a merchant, however rich, could be a gentleman. In the towns, the *bourgeoisie* – as it is called by some historians – comprised the merchants, craftsmen, semi-professionals like the law clerks, and the richer artisans. Here the wealthier citizens ruled their fellows, just as the gentry ruled the counties. The only other social group of any importance comprised the yeomanry and tenant farmers of the counties. In many areas the yeomanry were prospering and were often as rich as the lesser gentry. Inflation had reduced the value of the forty shilling freehold, fixed in the fifteenth century, so many yeomen and even some husbandmen had the right to vote. They shared with the lesser gentry the work of jurymen, churchwardens, constables and overseers of the poor. Some writers have seen their independence as the backbone of Puritanism and, later, the New Model Army (42).

At the bottom of society was the great majority who had neither political rights nor political consciousness; 'no account is made of them but only to be ruled, and not to rule other' (Sir Thomas Smith, 1565). The common people lived on the borderline of poverty and in hard times were kept from starvation, and possibly revolt, by handouts from private charity or the agencies of poor relief. Those who were dependent on the textile industry were particularly vulnerable.

Although historians echo seventeenth-century commentators when they see fairly precise differences of status among English people at this time, occupations were unspecialised and had less to do with social status than one might at first expect. Thus the nobleman ventured into mining; the merchant acquired an estate; the gentleman's younger son went into trade; the lawyer joined a trading company, and the yeoman farmer dabbled in some local industrial activity. By twentieth-century standards, movement between social groups was small; yet it happened. In England, wrote Thomas Fuller rather optimistically in 1642, 'the temple of honour is bolted against none'. Recently some writers have developed this theme of social mobility rather than class conflict, pointing to the tendency of some people of middle and lower status to move upward in the social hierarchy rather than seek power for their own class. Although this social mobility contributed to the vigour of national life, it did not, of course, alter the social framework **(47)**.

THE MACHINERY OF GOVERNMENT

By modern standards, the administrative system over which Robert Cecil presided from 1598 until 1612 was hardly a system at all. Yet, by seventeenth-century standards, James I inherited one of the best-governed states in Europe. A select and powerful Council advised the ruler, administered the realm, controlled the J.P.s, adjudicated on certain legal matters and managed the House of Commons. Two regional councils, in the North and in the Marches of Wales, combined administrative with legal duties and were agencies through which the central government sought to impose its will on the provinces. The key figures in local government were the justices of the peace, unpaid amateurs appointed by the king. A large and growing number of parliamentary statutes and executive instructions depended on the J.P.s for their enforcement. When parliament granted a subsidy, they would join with the sheriffs and officers of the towns in each county to form a special commission for the assessment and collection of taxes. In addition, they had extensive legal jurisdiction.

Throughout the sixteenth and early seventeenth centuries royal government meant, for most of the time, government without parliament; so much so that one historian has written of a decline of parliamentary government during this period **(93)**. During the period 1603 to 1629 parliament was in session for about three years and four months, approximately one eighth of the time. Yet if the government of England was the king's business, the importance and powers of parliament were well established. It gave advice, passed legislation and authorised taxation. The monarch, however, was vital to parliament's existence, for he alone could call, prorogue and dissolve it. His consent was needed before its statutes became law. Claiming to represent the nation, parliament really represented the landowning class. In a Lower House containing 475 members in 1614, all were landed gentry except 48 lawyers and 42 merchants. The right to vote in borough and parliamentary elections varied widely. In the counties, the franchise was limited to those owning freehold land worth forty shillings a year, but in some boroughs most householders had it, and in others only members of the corporation. According to Richard Baxter, inferior persons in the counties 'ordinarily choose such as their landlords do desire them to choose'. The privileges of the Commons, which to some extent protected them from royal interference, had grown during the sixteenth century but did not yet include the right to speak freely about everything. Certain subjects, such as foreign policy, were taboo. Like Elizabeth, James tried hard to maintain the Tudor definition of free speech which allowed members to discuss only those matters put before them by the government. Members enjoyed freedom from arrest during a session, though not after, and under James they managed to establish control over disputed elections. Although the privileges of the Commons enabled parliament to correct the errors of the government, they were not claimed as a matter of expediency, but of right. A parliament denied its privileges, it was said, was no parliament at all.

On the face of it, the House of Lords seems a much less important institution than the Commons. However, the recent publication of the *Parliamentary Journals* of 1610 has demonstrated that, in practice, parliament was not merely the House of Commons, but a single institution in which the Lords played a very important part (17). In 1603 there were 55 lay peers. James had increased them to 80 by 1610, 90 by 1621 and 96 by 1624. There were 24 bishops and 2 archbishops who, although not as important as in pre-Reformation times, were politically active, especially in committees. The peers spent much time on private business and parochial affairs. Usually the king could rely on the support of the Upper House, which generally exercised a moderating influence on the Commons. During the first parliament of the reign the government made extensive, though not very effective, use of conferences between the two Houses in an attempt to edge the Commons in the required direction. Occasionally, the two Houses cooperated. Together in 1621 they attacked the monopolists Mompesson and Mitchell and impeached Lord Chancellor Bacon. In 1624 they came together to impeach Lionel Cranfield. Cooperation with the Commons should not be equated with opposition to the king. The impeachments had tacit royal consent. Although there were individual peers like Lord Sheffield and the Earl of Southampton who, from factional jealousies, opposed the Crown, the majority showed a strong concern for royal interests and the prerogative.

The King of England in the seventeenth century appears at first sight to be absolute. He appointed and dismissed at will his councillors, judges and J.P.s. He settled all questions of policy, foreign and domestic, and could summon, prorogue and dismiss parliament when and as he pleased. In practice, however, there were considerable restrictions on his power. Every aspect of government was his personal concern, for which he paid the bills with revenues from Crown lands, the profits of justice, feudal payments such as fines and wardships, and customs duties which, by Tudor parliaments, had been granted to the monarch for life. When all the bills were paid, there was nothing left to maintain a standing army or even a police force, both necessary accompaniments to absolute rule. Another practical limitation on the king's power was his dependence on parliament's consent to direct taxation. Similarly, because English rulers had never been rich enough to establish a paid bureaucracy of local officials to govern the counties, they relied instead on the unpaid services of the peers and gentry of the shires, and the wealthy citizens of the towns. The king's authority was ultimately dependent on the cooperation of this ruling class.

THE ELIZABETHAN LEGACY

Although James I was spared some very difficult problems that faced Elizabeth at her accession, it is important to remember that many of the king's burdens were not of his own making. Such is the continuity between the reigns of Elizabeth and James that a study of the latter could well begin in 1588 rather than in 1603. There was continuity of men, institutions and problems. These years were marked by economic difficulties and continued inflation, by a decline in the standards of administrative efficiency and honesty; by financial difficulties and by constitutional conflict between Crown and Commons and religious disagreements between Anglicans and Puritans. Seventeenth-century writers like Thomas Wilson and John Aubrey were conscious of profound social and economic changes which seemed to sharpen political conflict. Modern writers have also traced the roots of seventeenth-century political conflict to sixteenth-century social change (66, 78). It was during James's reign that new ideas and social forces emerged which undermined the traditional order in Church and State alike, while the ending of war with Spain removed a unifying factor between ruler and ruled and encouraged demands for reform.

One very serious problem centred on the system of patronage that had developed during the sixteenth century (106). The administration was not conducted by a disinterested bureaucracy but by an underpaid civil service assisted by a volunteer army of unpaid officials. The Crown's authority was therefore dependent upon political persuasion, the basic ingredient of which was the reality or hope of reward. The main prizes were leases of Crown lands, *farms* (or leases) of various branches of the revenue, titles of honour, pensions, monopolies and offices. Because patronage involved the creation of a following, the system was not restricted to the monarch. Each great courtier built up a trelliswork of dependents by the giving or sale of favours. To supplement low salaries (or no salaries at all) various perquisites, schedules, fees and unofficial gratuities were levied. Thus between every suitor and his goal stood a crowd of middlemen with palms outstretched. Professor Hurstfield has estimated that when Elizabeth received about £650,000 from wardships during her reign, the purchasers of wardships and the lessees of the wards' lands had actually paid about £2 million – the difference going to those officials who stood between the suitors and their Queen (**45**, p. 345). Corruption is a vague and subjective charge. There was nothing inherently decadent about patronage; 'it was a system of rule appropriate for its day' (**96**, p. 134). Yet the system had a number of unfortunate effects which grew more pronounced as the years advanced. Because there were never enough offices to go round, entirely new offices were created in an attempt to meet demand. It was not easy for king and Council to receive disinterested advice when loyalty was conditioned by the hope of reward. Administrative and financial reforms were difficult because they threatened to disturb a vast network of vested interests. The system also helped to perpetuate the disease of factional strife in English government; as one family or group struggled for influence over the king, their clients struggled too, and were resisted by those who stood to lose power and place.

James, at his accession, had not so serious a religious problem as Elizabeth faced at hers. By 1603 the Church of England was firmly established. The Puritan challenge to its government and liturgy had been repulsed and the majority of Englishmen seemed content to accept it as part of the system of government (**32**). The irreconcilables – Catholics and Puritans – were a small, if important, minority. Like most rulers of this period, James believed that all his subjects should be members of the state Church. Nonconformity was not only an affront to God but a threat to the unity of the kingdom. The main problem confronting James was how to deal with the Catholics without driving them to rebellion or conspiracy, and how to persuade the Puritans to accept the organisation and practices of the state Church without disrupting that Church by violent controversy. Another problem was the poverty of the Church and especially of the parish clergy. The Church under Elizabeth had been unmercifully plundered. Elizabeth had 'encouraged' her bishops to part with their choicest lands. While the value of bishoprics declined, the expenses of a bishop were increasing. In a period of inflation, the bishops had to provide not only for themselves and their households, but for wives and families as well. So they too plundered the Church, selling timber and other resources to raise capital, and giving their relatives long leases of episcopal lands on favourable terms. Elizabeth had backed the high episcopal party of Archbishop Whitgift and set her face against concessions to even the most moderate of the Puritans, with the result that pressures for reform were dammed up only to burst upon James in the next century. The Elizabethan bishops had achieved some small success in raising the educational standards of the rural clergy, but there was still much to be done in this respect. Little could be done about the apathy and ignorance of many of the clergy until the wealth of the Church was increased, enabling it to attract and hold men of high calibre. Although the House of Commons was zealous in campaigning for a better ministry, the remedy was partly in its own hands since more than forty per cent of ecclesiastical livings were under the control of laymen (**41**). Something also needed to be done about abuses like pluralism and non-residence, problems that went back long before the Reformation. Although James put an end to the alienation of ecclesiastical revenues, there was no simple answer to the other problems (see ch. 6).

Probably the most serious difficulties James had to face stemmed from his government's insolvency. Allowing for differences in size and population the total gross income available to an English king was small compared with his French equivalent (**56**). Existing revenues were inelastic and new revenues difficult to find. Elizabeth, by remorseless economies and a minimum of foreign entanglements, had managed to avoid yawning deficits. This achievement was undermined by the long war with Spain. Rather than persuade parliament to provide greater and more regular revenues, the Queen preferred to sell land. By 1603 there was little room for manoeuvre, for without parliamentary subsidies money could only be raised from monopolies, impositions and the like. Customs farming and the sale of offices, monopolies and wardships brought money to the Crown at the same time as it transferred the cost of administration to the subject. It also distorted the economy and provided parliament with a fertile crop of complaints. Yet so long as the king lacked adequate revenues and a salaried civil service, there was little else he could do. In truth, the English State was ceasing to be viable without some radical reform of the existing financial structure. As the Crown grew poorer, parliament was able to tighten its grip on the revenue system because it possessed the power of consent to most taxation; and because parliament paid the piper, it tried to call the tune. James had thus to face the wellnigh insuperable problem of raising extra revenue while resisting the encroachments of parliament on the royal prerogative.

The accession of a new king seemed a good time to seek a clearer definition of the constitutional situation. Could parliament legitimately attack an official of the Crown? Had the king the right to silence criticism or collect 'unparliamentary' revenues such as impositions?

Someone, of course, had to decide. The judges were an obvious choice, but they invariably decided for the Crown, so that legally upheld interpretations of the prerogative appeared to interfere with the rights of the subject, as when the Exchequer Court decreed in 1606 that the king could impose an additional customs duty on currants. Sir Edward Coke, after he had angered the king by championing the common law courts against High Commission and by opposing James's use of proclamations, propounded a doctrine of the supremacy of the common law. In 1607, according to his own account, he told James bluntly that 'his majesty was not learned in the laws of England', and that English kings were under the law. Coke is a complex man, whose motives are difficult to explain; his views cannot be put explicitly and are a matter of controversy. But he did set up the common law as a bulwark against what he regarded as the authoritarian tendencies of the Stuarts. To Coke the law was sovereign, and he envisaged the judiciary as a kind of supreme court, adjudicating constitutional disputes (11). After 1616, having been dismissed from the Bench, Coke tended to exalt the authority of parliament which, by a piece of legal antiquarianism, he regarded as the court at the summit of the common law. Despite the obscurities and inconsistencies of his arguments, Coke's insistence that the common law protected the subject against the encroachments of the monarchy became part of the parliamentary tradition (104). In parliament itself, M.P.s believed that king and parliament were integral parts of a balanced constitution (46). The effectiveness of government depended on harmony and consent, on keeping the constitution in balance. The belief that the prerogatives of the Crown were balanced by the rights of the subject was a pious hope, not an accurate political assessment, for the balance of the constitution was already upset when James ascended the throne. On the one hand, parliament's importance had increased; on the other, the powers of the king had grown. The Crown had taken over the headship of the Church; it had enlarged the sphere of its activities and increased both the extent and effectiveness of its powers. At the same time, the Crown's financial predicament made it increasingly dependent on a parliament impelled to make such claims for itself that the traditional prerogatives of the monarch were seriously threatened. Thus the vision of the 'ancient constitution' served only to hide the facts of life; as a concept, it was unworkable. Yet its existence encouraged a search for scapegoats when disharmony prevailed, and discouraged any serious attempt to face the practical problem of how disagreement between king and parliament might be resolved.

If James I's difficulties were considerable, so were the expectations of his subjects. Puritans hoped for reform of the Church, Papists for toleration and lower recusancy fines. The king's ministers hoped to increase his revenues, while his people expected a reduction of taxation when peace was made with Spain. Members of parliament who, in 1604 claimed falsely to have neglected to press their grievances during the twilight years of Elizabeth's reign 'in regard to her sex and age', expected satisfaction from James. In such a situation only a ruler of genius would have enjoyed a highly successful reign. There is no unanimity among historians, however, about the seriousness of the situation in 1603. Professor Elton has impatiently rejected the habit of placing emphasis on the problems inherited by James as if 'only James I ever had problems. Even the emphatic demonstration that he either created his own or was responsible for making existing ones insoluble has not disposed of the general notion that in some way the situation was past praying for in 1603' (87, p. 327). If, of course, there is nothing about the state of affairs with which someone like Elizabeth could not have coped, then the dramatic deterioration in the political situation after 1603 must be due largely to the incompetence and extravagance of King James. Professor Donaldson, impressed by James's record as ruler of Scotland, is one historian who emphasises the difficulties of the Elizabethan legacy, arguing that

'the cares and burdens were not of James's making; they constituted the *damnosa hereditas* left by Elizabeth Tudor, a sovereign utterly careless of the well-being of her kingdom after her own demise, who had allowed unsolved problems to pile up in her later years and whose reign had ended in anti-climax, in decline, almost in failure. James went to a country heading for insolvency, and one in which the whole system of government was already being challenged. . . . He tried to apply in England the same principles of authoritarianism and pacification as he had applied in Scotland. . . . His logic and commonsense were not appreciated by his more emotional English subjects, but the fact is that problems which Gloriana never solved were solved by this king from Scotland' (34, p. 236-7).

PART TWO

Analysis

3   Finance: The Canker of Want

ROYAL EXTRAVAGANCE

The most crippling problem that James had to face was the insolvency of the Crown. Policies, if they are to be effective, need money. Yet the king of England never had enough to make ends meet, dependent as he was on a financial system that was a relic of creaking antiquity and dangerous inadequacy. Like his medieval predecessors, James I was expected to 'live of his own' and pay the crippling costs of kingship from his ordinary revenue, which consisted of the receipts from Crown lands and customs, and such items as feudal revenues, profits of justice, clerical taxation and penal taxation on recusants. 'Extraordinary' revenues from parliament helped cover the cost of abnormal situations like a war, a coronation or a royal funeral. The tax on land voted in parliament and called a subsidy was collected at the rate of 4s in the £ of a man's assessed income. The country as a whole, and the peerage in particular, was undertaxed. 'The Englishman', said Francis Bacon, 'is most master of his own valuation and the least bitten of any nation in Europe.' Assessments for taxation, carried out by special commissions, had been realistic during the reign of Henry VIII but became progressively less so as the sixteenth century advanced, due largely to the difficulty of making continual revaluations to offset the ravages of inflation. There was no improvement under James. Buckingham was assessed at £400 when his income, in 1623, was about £15,000. The gentry, too, were undertaxed. In Sussex the average sum at which seventy-eight families were assessed fell from £48 each in 1560 to £14 in 1626 (105). While the propertied classes grew wealthier, the government was unable to tax this wealth and acquire a settled income from regular taxation. A century of inflation lay at the root of the Crown's financial difficulties. While the cost of government surged ahead, the King's income limped behind. As James wrote to his Council in 1607: 'The only disease and consumption which I can ever apprehend as likeliest to endanger me is this canker of want, which being removed, I could think myself as happy in all other respects as any other King or Monarch that ever was since the birth of Christ.' The Government's poverty made the Crown increasingly dependent on the London money market (26). It was to a small group of financiers that the King applied for loans, for unlike Elizabeth, James did not live in terror of debt. These men lent large sums of money on the security of the customs, which they were then allowed to collect.

Rising prices, the inability of parliament to recognise changing economic conditions, the reluctance of landowners to pay for the increased cost of government with heavier taxation, the additional household expenses of a monarch with a wife and children, all these are weighty reasons why James found it impossible to pay his way. Elizabeth had managed only by a degree of parsimony which created as many problems as it solved. The financial system was clearly outdated and it was high time that parliament faced this unpalatable fact. Unfortunately, the chances of their doing so were reduced by the king's carefree extravagance. James I was congenitally incapable of thrift. His reckless prodigality was cited by both Sir Walter Raleigh and Sir Thomas Lake as one of the main causes of his trouble with parliament. After years of excruciating penury in Scotland, the king's urge to give and spend freely is understandable. He was encouraged to be generous by a noisy chorus of courtiers, some of whom should have known better. The Council argued, with some truth, that royal generosity would 'multiply and confirm affection and duty'. Bacon in 1612, as a member of a Treasury Commission charged with reducing the debt, wrote cheerfully to James that 'it is no new thing for the greatest of kings to be in debt', and hoped that 'these cogitations of want' would not 'vex your Majesty's mind'.

From the beginning James was expected to be, and was, generous. The English court had embarked on an orgy of extravagance long before its new king had arrived, panting to participate, from the north. But whereas Elizabeth had refused to open her purse for the benefit of all, James was flattered into playing a major role in the riot of un-bridled expenditure. 'To what an immense Riches in his time did the Merchandise of England rise to above former Ages? intoned Hacket. What Buildings? What Sumptuousness? What Feastings? What gorgeous Attire? What massy Plate and Jewels? What prodigal Marriage Portions were grown in fashion among the Nobility and Gentry, as if the Skies Rained Plenty?' (8, i, 224). Soon after James's accession the Earl of Shrewsbury was heard to remark with satisfaction that Elizabeth 'valued every molehill that she gave . . . at a mountain, which our sovereign now does not'. Money, Crown lands, leases, offices, wardships and titles fell in a golden rain on the heads of the parched nobility and gentry. The king's prodigality is recorded in the Exchequer accounts. In 1603 'diverse causes and rewards' amounted to £11,741; in 1604,

£18,510 and by 1605, £35,239. 'Fees and annuities' paid out to courtiers accounted for £27,270 in 1603, £34,593 in 1604 and £47,783 in 1605. In that year a commission reporting on the state of the finances declared that 'the empty places of that glorious garland of your crown cannot be repaired when the garden of your Majesty's Treasure shall be made a common pasture for all that are in need or have unreasonable desires'. James took little notice of such warnings, reserving the full force of his generosity for those fortunate individuals who took his fancy. Happy indeed were they whom the king delighted to honour. First Robert Carr, and then George Villiers, owed their great wealth to the king's liberality. James gave away so much that it is sometimes wondered if he appreciated the value of money. One story, almost certainly exaggerated, tells how Cecil, having been instructed to pay out some £20,000 to a favourite, stacked the coin into a great pile at a place where the king would pass and perhaps realise how great a sum it was. 'Thereupon the king fell into a passion, protesting he was abused, never intending any such gift: And casting himself upon the heap scrabbled out the quantity of two or three hundred pounds, and swore that he should have no more' (**21**, i, 231-3).

Elizabeth's ordinary expenditure had normally settled at about £300,000 a year: James was soon spending half a million pounds annually. This increase was partly because James, unlike his predecessor, had a family to provide for, each with a separate household. As the centre of government, the court had to be magnificent enough to impress foreign envoys. Yet provision was made beyond the bounds of reason [**doc. 4**]. The Wardrobe account, which had averaged £9,535 in the last four years of Elizabeth's reign, jumped to an average of £36,377 in the first five years of James's reign. The number of ushers, grooms, carvers, cup-bearers, pages, messengers, gentlemen of the bedchamber and the privy chamber multiplied alarmingly. Gentlemen of the privy chamber, for instance, increased from eighteen in 1603 to forty-eight in 1624, while 200 gentlemen extraordinary were added to the court, all consuming food and fuel at the king's expense and vying with one another in pilfering his palaces. Festivities were numerous and opulent. When in 1613 the Treasury was empty, James managed to raise £93,000 to spend on the marriage of his daughter to Frederick of the Palatinate. The king loved the rowdy companionship of great feasts and delighted in gambling; the queen had an unquenchable thirst for amateur theatricals. These expensive entertainments, called masques, were polished to perfection by Ben Jonson and Inigo Jones and became one of the characteristic features of the Jacobean court. In old age James began to realise how dangerous was his extravagance. By then it was too late; the habits and style of himself and his court had become engrained, and a burden of debt established that was not the result of military necessity, as under Elizabeth, but of the king's incorrigible bounty (33).

ATTEMPTS TO IMPROVE THE FINANCES

Recent studies of Jacobean finance have emphasised that the financial situation at the beginning of the reign was far from hopeless (59). The debt of £400,000 bequeathed by Elizabeth was largely covered by the £300,000 granted by parliament in 1601, which was still coming in. Substantial economies were effected when Ireland was pacified and the war with Spain ended. Whereas Ireland cost Elizabeth £342,074 for the year ending at Michaelmas 1602, it cost James only £38,251 for a similar period in 1607. With England and Scotland under the same sovereign, the cost of garrisoning the border was also reduced. James should have been able to balance his accounts, but was unable to do so because he was extravagant and reluctant to face the drudgery of administrative supervision.

This analysis, which makes James primarily responsible for the government's insolvency, does not make much allowance for problems and weaknesses inherent in the administrative system of early Stuart England. Although it is true that economies would have made some difference to the Crown's financial position, it can be argued that, in the long term, a dramatic improvement was impossible without a radical revision of the whole financial system designed to provide the Crown with the benefits of regular taxation. Existing revenues barely covered the costs of government and were alarmingly inelastic. Attempts to stretch the framework by, for example, levying impositions, led to accusations of illegality from parliament. The need to raise a definite revenue by farming the customs, the granting of pensions, the taking of bribes, the levying of wardships and purveyance, all stemmed· from fundamental weaknesses in the financial system inherited by the Stuarts. The entrenched interests of parliament, courtiers and officials in the existing system made it extremely difficult for a reforming minister to carry out any lasting improvement. 'Deeper still', writes Professor Hurstfield, 'lay the whole complex of weaknesses throughout the government machine: duplication, amateurishness, defalcation, the lack of able and committed administrators of the middle rank to hold departments together and loyally to carry out the policy set forth by the Lord Treasurer' (95, p. 240). If it is agreed that the financial system which James inherited was no longer viable, then his extravagance becomes not the prime cause of the government's difficulties but only an aggravating factor. Perhaps the most significant consequence of the king's behaviour was that it became difficult to persuade parliament that government could not be financed from the king's ordinary income unless it was dramatically increased.

The work of the first Lord Treasurer, the Earl of Dorset, was confined to enlarging and husbanding royal resources. In an attempt to secure a steady income from customs, he and Robert Cecil decided to abandon the direct administration of these revenues and return to a system whereby the rights of collection were leased to a group of financiers. At a time when so much else concerning the king's revenue was uncertain, the establishment of the Great Farm of the Customs provided the Treasury with exact knowledge of how much to expect from customs. In addition, loans could be raised in anticipation of revenue, an inestimable advantage to the poverty stricken government (26). So, for the first time since the reign of Mary, a new schedule of import and export duties was compiled. After months of negotiations the Great Farm was sold to a syndicate of merchants in December 1604. For seven years they could collect all the duties, except those specifically excluded (like the duties on wine and currants), in return for £112,400 a year. Despite such measures, Dorset could never raise enough money to balance the accounts, so the government had to run on credit. When he died in 1608 the debt from accumulated deficits amounted to over half a million.

One reason why the financial position of the Crown did not improve was because no effort had been made to persuade parliament to review the taxation system. Because Elizabeth had vigorously exploited a variety of non-parliamentary sources of revenue such as wardship, purveyance and the sale of monopolies, parliament was in no mood to negotiate. An attempt to reach a settlement was made in 1610, two years after the appointment as Treasurer of the Earl of Salisbury, a man determined to expand the king's revenues. Salisbury was inhibited from launching a very necessary programme of retrenchment and reform by his own involvement in the sharp practices and profiteering of the court. As Master of the Wards he pocketed large sums of money; as Treasurer he used the customs farms as bait to hook gifts and private loans. In an admittedly short span of office he failed to bring about any dramatic improvement in the financial situation. In 1608 the deficit was £178,000; in 1612, when he died, it was £160,000. The debt when he took over was £597,337; it was £500,000 four years later despite the sale of Crown land worth £432,651 (59). These figures do Salisbury less than justice. While growing rich in the royal service he sacrificed his health, and ultimately his popularity with the king, by attempting to drive through parliament a major financial reform which, if successful, would have done much to improve the finances.

Salisbury began by instituting a thorough survey of Crown lands, selecting the least profitable for sale. This sale of land and woods raised £445,000 but lost the Exchequer over £14,500 worth of rent each year. Attempts to secure a more economic return from royal estates, by increasing rents and improving standards of stewardship, were not very successful, largely because of difficulties of supervision. In spite of these measures, the gap between income and expenditure that caused the debt could not be closed. To tide over the annual deficit, money had to be borrowed, usually at 10 per cent. Consequently a substantial and, if possible, permanent increase in revenue was needed. The Lord Treasurer sought to obtain such an increase in two ways: first, by expanding income from customs, and second, by trying to persuade parliament to provide the king with an annual income. Unfortunately, the success of the first scheme prejudiced the success of the second.

In 1608 Salisbury issued a new Book of Rates which increased customs tariffs and levied impositions, or extra duties, on a wide variety of merchandise. Dorset had taken hesitant steps in the same direction but had been resisted by John Bate, a London merchant who refused to pay an imposition on currants. In 1606 James sued Bate in the Exchequer court and won his case. On the strength of this decision, Salisbury levied impositions on 1,400 articles, excluding basic foodstuffs and munitions. The Treasurer hoped thereby to raise £60,000, a figure strikingly close to the £59,000 which Cranfield in 1613 estimated was lost to the Crown by grants and cheap leases to courtiers. Although it took six years to raise the rent of the Great Farm to correspond with the increases, Salisbury had hit on a most fruitful way of increasing revenue. Sir Julius Caesar wrote of Salisbury's impositions that they 'will prove the most gainful to the king and his posterity of any one day's work by any Lord Treasurer since the time of King Edward III' (33, ii, 120). Caesar was right; by the late 1630s impositions were bringing in £218,000 a year. Their immediate effect, however, was to raise a storm of protest in the Commons, where some members feared that the Crown would use and extend such financial devices to establish despotic government.

The uproar over impositions came at a time when Salisbury was attempting to put into practice the second half of his plan to increase ordinary revenue. This proposal, called the Great Contract, was the only attempt during the reign of James to get at the root of the financial difficulties of the Crown, which stemmed from the archaic principle that the king should live of his own. Salisbury tried to persuade the Commons that the king's commitments were no longer covered by his real income, which had fallen disastrously. Parliament was asked to 'support' the Crown with £200,000 per annum. After some hard bargaining the Commons consented, while the king agreed to abandon wardship and purveyance and to enforce the penal laws. When parliament adjourned in July 1610 it looked as if Salisbury had successfully procured a fiscal reform of considerable magnitude, similar to that made at the Restoration in 1660. But after the recess, as a result of widespread anxiety about the radicalism of the proposal, the Great Contract collapsed (p. 42).

Salisbury continued as Treasurer until his death in 1612. In the royal household a few economies were made, but lack of support from the king, and the entrenched self-interest of officials, prevented any startling improvement. Mrs Prestwich, in her biography of Cranfield, has criticised severely Salisbury's policies as Treasurer, which she claims were motivated by weakness, fear and greed (59, pp. 19-48). His failure to combat corruption, curb royal extravagance and introduce economies prevented the elimination of the recurring deficits that stopped the debt being cleared. Since the ruthless application of a policy of retrenchment and administrative reform could lead to political suicide, it is not surprising that Salisbury avoided grasping the nettle of corruption. It was, perhaps, more realistic to introduce impositions and to fish for new taxes than to mount an attack on the excessive cost of administration.

HARD TIMES: 1612-1621

Between Salisbury's death and Cranfield's appointment as Lord Treasurer in 1621 there was an interlude of financial ineptitude, brightened only by a largely unsuccessful attempt to improve the situation in 1617 [doc. 5]. The government tried a number of money-raising devices, the most important being the sale of titles of honour. Professor Lawrence Stone, in his superb analysis of this venture, has concluded that 'the *minimum* profits from the sale of all honours between 1603 and 1629 is . . . about £620,000' (65, p. 127). James and his Council began by selling knighthoods, and then invented a new hereditary title of baronet, which was bestowed on gentlemen prepared to pay £1,095. Between 1611 and 1614 £90,885 was collected in this way and put to good use, helping to meet the cost of maintaining an army in Ireland. Although James kept a promise not to create more than 200 baronets, the free sale of the title inevitably diminished the honour in the eyes of both the public and potential buyers. The price fell accordingly, from £1,098 in 1611 to £700 in 1619, and to £220 in 1622. In 1615, desperate for money after the failure of the 1614 parliament, advised by Bacon and encouraged by the Villiers family, James assented to the marketing of peerages. Between December 1615 and December 1628 the peerage expanded from 81 to 126, while the number of earls increased from 27 to 65. Some payments were earmarked for specific purposes. When, for instance, £30,000 was required in 1624 to help pay the cost of Buckingham's embassy to Paris, the money was raised by a sale of peerages. However, much of the money raised in this way dropped straight into the pockets of courtiers. Such a sale of honours, while supplementing royal revenues, inevitably brought the Crown and aristocracy into disrepute.

Another scheme for raising revenue brought James nothing but trouble. In December 1614 the king allowed Alderman Sir William Cockayne, a rich merchant and Crown creditor, to launch a project designed to boost the earnings of those involved in the manufacture and export of cloth. It is difficult to decide whether the plan was simply a failure or a barefaced fraud. Cockayne argued that since over half England's exported cloth was unfinished, it would be very profitable to forbid the export of undyed cloth, setting up instead a dyeing industry to do the job at home. The government was promised an annual revenue of £40,000 from increased customs and from the import of dyestuffs. When in December 1614 James withdrew the charter of the Merchant Adventurers, Cockayne and his colleagues acquired control of the profitable export trade to Germany and the Low countries. The new company soon showed its true colours. In 1615 it received permission to export unfinished cloth, ostensibly because Cockayne was as yet unable to find either the capital or the skills required for a large-scale expansion of the finishing process. Sir William, it seemed, was less interested in improving the cloth industry than in snatching from the Merchant Adventurers their virtual monopoly of the export of cloth. By 1616 it was clear that Cockayne lacked the capital to fulfil the obligation, hitherto fulfilled by the Adventurers, to buy cloth from the clothing districts and hold it until it could be marketed. The crash came when the Dutch retaliated by prohibiting the import of any English cloth, finished or not. The company limped on for another year while stocks piled up, men went bankrupt, the weavers of Wiltshire and Gloucestershire rioted, cloth exports slumped and the industry stagnated. In 1617 the king abandoned Cockayne, and the Merchant Adventurers, having distributed between £70,000 and £80,000 in bribes, had their privileges restored. Although Cockayne's project did not cause the depression of 1620, it probably contributed to the resentment of merchants and clothiers at government economic interference (35, 67).

Although new revenue could not easily be found, existing revenue could be made to go further. When, after 1615, the Crown experienced some difficulty in raising loans, the Council began to work for a surplus on the ordinary account which could be used to pay off royal debts. The various departments of state were told to cut their expenses, but because they were left to devise their own economies, little was achieved. Late in 1617 the Council commissioned Lionel Cranfield, a talented and dynamic London merchant and Surveyor General of the Customs, to supervise the inauguration of a more severe régime. Cranfield at once took a pruning knife to the administration of the royal household which, in 1617, cost James £77,630. After a hard struggle a saving of £18,000 was achieved. It was 'the first effective effort of the Stuart period to improve Crown finances' (**59**, p. 211). Gradually, the economies were extended along a broader front. In July 1618 Lord Treasurer Suffolk, charged with corruption, was dismissed and the Treasury put under the control of a number of commissioners. The retrenchment which they and Cranfield carried out was not a spectacular success, but at a time when the king was dangerously over-spending, it helped to avert a financial crisis. The commissioners saved about £85,000 a year by pruning the expenditure of the Household, Wardrobe, Navy and Ordnance. They increased revenue by about £36,000 a year by stepping up the returns from the Wards, by revising the customs farms and extending impositions. These attempts at reform show that something could be done within the antiquated system of finance to cut expenditure and increase revenue. Yet, although the commissioners managed by 1619 almost to balance the ordinary account, there was not enough money to wipe out the king's debts which, in 1620, were approaching £900,000. James had made no effort to limit his thoughtless extravagance or to reduce the pension list, which in two decades had become a major source of financial weakness.

LIONEL CRANFIELD, EARL OF MIDDLESEX, LORD TREASURER 1621-1624

In 1621 Cranfield began the final and most determined attempt to solve the king's financial problems. There was nothing creative or revolution-ary about his methods; he simply transferred to the larger theatre of affairs of state the lessons he had learnt in business. Having called a halt to borrowing and to the indiscriminate sale of Crown lands, he tried to screw as much money as possible from existing revenues. Customs were an obvious target. There was little chance of any radical improvement here, however, because of the trade depression. Determined to enlarge the king's share of the takings of the tax farmers, Cranfield persuaded them to agree to a £4,000 increase in rent. Much of the Treasurer's energies were devoted to a grim assault on administrative costs and the profits of office. Government departments were ordered to be thrifty and to put their balance sheets in order. Military outlay in Ireland and the United Provinces was cut and an attempt made to force up revenue from such resources as wardships and debts owed to the Crown. He cut savagely at the payment of gifts and pensions amidst screams of anguish from the court. He made powerful enemies. 'But the fact that the courtiers, backed by injured office holders, felt it imperative to unseat him is proof of his drive and determination' (**59**, p. 330). While Cranfield laboured to spend less, James was busy spending more. Perhaps because he had heard it all before, the king did not take too seriously his Treasurer's portentous memoranda about a financial crisis. Although Cranfield had suspended the payment of pensions, James and Buckingham were still prepared 'to float argosies'. Intending to stop the indiscriminate distributions of royal bounty, and to shelter the king from the bombardment of importunity, Cranfield obtained from James, in October 1622, a declaration that no grants of land, pensions, or allowances would be made without Treasury approval. No sooner was the ink dry than James was making exceptions, especially for Buckingham, who needed £30,000 for a new house at Burley.

By 1623 the tide was running strongly against Cranfield. Within a year he had been drowned by a huge wave of expenditure on foreign policy, as the Bohemian crisis led the king to spend lavishly on ambassadors and secret agents, and on the revival of the navy. The figures speak for themselves: the cost of foreign and defence services in 1618-19 had been respectively £16,400 and £42,600. The corresponding figures in 1620-21 were £58,900 and £64,000; by 1621-22 they had risen to £79,000 and £98,800 (**68**, p. 212). All the money that was saved by Cranfield's remorseless economies was gobbled up by this increased expenditure. In 1623 Charles and Buckingham went to Madrid to arrange a Spanish marriage (see Ch. 8). Their escapade was a diplomatic and financial disaster, their seven-month stay in Madrid alone costing £46,668. When, in 1624, Cranfield opposed war against Spain, Buckingham turned against him and let loose on him the pack of hungry courtiers whom the Treasurer had starved of the rewards of office. So, despite the tremendous drive behind his policies as Treasurer, Cranfield failed to make James solvent. In an age of personal monarchy, he could not hope to do so if the monarch declined to cooperate. James's support of Cranfield's measures had been, at best, half-hearted. By striking at office holders and by opposing the favourite the Treasurer had committed political suicide. The reasons for his failure go deeper. Cranfield was ultimately defeated by entrenched interests and by forces over which he had little or no control. An attempt to collect some of the arrears and debts owed to the Crown, estimated in 1621 to be worth £1,624,523, failed because the debtors resisted. Economies were fought at every level of the administration and collapsed dramatically as the storm gathered on the Continent. Cranfield's successor, Sir James Ley, husband of Buckingham's niece, was at once faced with a debt of one million pounds. The reign ended gloomily with the financial problem no nearer solution, the government becoming fatally dependent on what Cranfield called 'shifts and bargains'. Under Charles I, such schemes — monopolies, ship money, impositions and the like — were, according to Clarendon 'every day set on foot for money, which served only to offend and insense the people, and brought little supply to the king's occasions' (**4**, i, 32).

4   Crown and Parliament

CONFLICT BETWEEN KING AND COMMONS

James made many difficulties for himself, but one of his greatest problems, an aggressive House of Commons, was an embarrassing legacy from his predecessor. The view that parliament, despite its growing strength, was in basic harmony with the Crown under the Tudors, only to become suddenly assertive under the Stuarts, has now been revised. Although there was not one session during her long reign when a clash between Elizabeth and some members of the Commons did not occur, serious trouble was usually avoided by a skilful exercise of the arts of parliamentary management by the queen and her privy councillors. The proliferation of committees, however, reduced the influence of the councillors, while the invention, in 1606, of the Committee of the Whole House enabled the Commons to replace the Speaker, a royal nominee, with their own chairman (107). Handpicked subcommittees were appointed by the Committee of the Whole House as spearheads of the campaign against grievances. Although the diarists of the Jacobean parliaments pass over these procedural developments and concentrate on the clash of personalities and policies, the Commons' businesslike investigation of abuses helped to make opposition to the Crown very effective.

James I's failure to provide a team of privy councillors able to make a satisfactory show of parliamentary management is usually cited as a main reason why he had difficulty with the Commons (76). The explanation is sound, as far as it goes, though it needs some qualification. The success of Elizabeth's councillors in managing parliament was partly a result of the broad sympathy that existed between them and the backbenchers in the Commons. Moderate Puritan councillors like Sir Francis Knollys and Sir Walter Mildmay had often supported measures which were unpalatable to the queen. As this generation died out, they were replaced by men who were less successful at persuading the House to do as the government wished. Some of these men were secondrate: Sir John Fortescue, or Mr Secretary Herbert who became known in James's reign as Mr Secondary Herbert. The general decline in the character of the Council began before James ascended the throne.

Not only did he fail to arrest this decline, he also failed to maintain the exclusiveness of the Elizabethan Council. In 1610 there were twenty members: in 1615 twenty-four. By 1618 membership had risen to thirty-one, and stood around thirty-five from 1620 to 1625. If there were too many councillors at court, there were not enough in the Commons. During the first parliament there were two or three councillors in the Lower House, and only four during the second. This was partly Robert Cecil's fault: he preferred to manage the Commons from the Lords by the use of conferences between the two Houses. Yet, since in 1621 and 1624 the government was careful to prepare a programme of legislation, using the councillors to pilot it through the Commons, the Crown's difficulties with parliament cannot be ascribed entirely to a failure of management (**61, 79**).

The councillors in the Commons were leaders of a substantial group of members associated in various ways with the Crown, who nevertheless failed consistently to defend government policies. Most of them kept silent, either because they sympathised with the complaints of the opposition, or because they had grievances of their own (**55, 76**). Very often they sensed the futility of resisting the more outspoken critics of the government. Their effectiveness was also hampered by factional struggles at court. In 1614 Sir Ralph Winwood, the Secretary of State, was opposed by the Howard family and his work in the Commons was sabotaged by disappointed contenders for the Secretaryship like Herbert, Lake and Caesar. In the same parliament, the Earl of Northampton 'set up a kind of flag unto all those that . . . would frustrate the success of this parliament' (**55**). Afterwards, Sir Francis Bacon advised James

to extinguish or at least compose for a time, the division in his own house, which otherwise . . . will be sure to have such influence and infusion into the House or perhaps the Houses of Parliament, as we shall only grow and profit in inconvenience. . . . Therefore it must be so handled that factions be so mortified, or at least laid asleep, that all do counsel a Parliament and come cheerfully to it (**59**, p. 137).

In 1621 a faction at court hostile to Lord Chancellor Bacon encouraged the opposition in the Commons to destroy him. In 1624 the Duke of Buckingham went into partnership with the opposition to do the same to Lord Treasurer Cranfield. Thus 'court faction, already a cause of instability in the Privy Council of Elizabeth, injected its poison into Parliament' (**59**, p. 136).

THE 'OPPOSITION'

Another cause of James's parliamentary troubles was the emergence in the Commons of an ill-defined but identifiable group of people critical of the court. Never more than forty in a House of 475, they exercised an influence out of all proportion to their numbers. It is easy to exaggerate the organisation and consistency of this 'Country' opposition to the Stuarts (54). Modern notions of 'party' cannot be applied to the actions of its so-called leaders. Take, for example, Dudley Digges, who attacked the government in the parliaments of 1614 and 1621, yet went abroad on business for the king in 1618 and 1620. In 1622 he was appointed to the Commission for Irish Revenues, but having failed thereafter to secure the patronage of Buckingham, he helped with the impeachment of the Duke in 1626 and with the formulation of the Petition of Right in 1628. In the 1630s he obtained the Mastership of the Rolls and a post on High Commission. Digges is not unique; inside almost every opponent of the Crown was a courtier struggling to get out. Nicholas Hyde abandoned opposition to become first a judge and then the chief justice who gave a verdict for Charles I in the Five Knights' Case. John Hoskyns, a Middle Temple lawyer, attacked impositions, the Scottish favourites and corruption at court in the parliament of 1610. By 1614 he had secured the patronage of the Howards and at their instruction precipitated a dissolution by attacking the favourites. William Hakewill was another lawyer prominent in opposition in 1610 and 1614. Yet by 1617 Bacon was able to write: 'The Queen hath made Mr Hakewill her solicitor. . . . He was an opposite in Parliament, as Jones was, that the King hath made Chief Justice of Ireland. But I hold it no ill counsel to win or remove such men.' William Noy, a critic of the court in the 'twenties, became Attorney General in the 'thirties. These men were not apostates, but realists. Although they attacked the court they were prepared to join it, not only for reward but for power, which they sincerely believed they would exercise better than their predessors.

To criticise the government effectively, M.P.s must have coordinated their activities, talking parliamentary business after hours and meeting informally to devise ways of thwarting the court. Nevertheless, it is impossible to demonstrate that the opponents of the court worked together as a team. Although they were as active in committee as on the floor of the House, they did not use the committee system as part of a carefully worked out strategy for winning control of the Commons. Their activities, which tended to work against royal interests, followed naturally on the procedural developments that were taking place as committees expanded in number and size. Sometimes they were overwhelmed by those they hoped to lead. In 1614, for example, opposition was so ill-directed that Digges, Fuller, Hakewill, Edwin Sandys and Wentworth lost control and the patients took over the asylum. Some M.P.s found opposition as sure a ladder to the plums of office as the patronage of the great. Others were spokesmen of particular vested interests. Sir Edwin Sandys, for instance, worked hard to benefit the Virginia Company whose treasurer he was, and whose trading interests in the New World gave it a sharp anti-Spanish axe to grind. In 1621 its spokesmen in the Commons were Sandys, Digges, John Ferrar and John Smyth, while the Earls of Warwick and Southampton were active on its behalf in the Lords. Their activities confirm Gondomar's warning to James that the Company 'would prove a seminary for a seditious parliament' (**59**, p. 305). The value of the Company's £12.50 shares having dropped to £2, Sandys and his colleagues tried to improve their affairs by persuading the Commons to recommend a ban on imported Spanish tobacco, leaving the market wide open for their own inferior yet more expensive product. So, if by the 1620s it is possible to identify an opposition, called by contemporaries *the Country*, based on principles that were conservative and constitutionally anachronistic, and united by a distrust of the court, this opposition was neither systematically organised nor disinterestedly led. While *Country* 'stood for certain policies and opinions which it sought to carry into public life' (**78**, p. 75), the word had an older meaning synonymous with county, a use of the word that would have won an immediate response from most M.P.s. The interests of most Englishmen were still concentrated on local rather than national affairs. This helps to explain why a man like Sir Robert Phelips, a leading political figure in Somerset, could display such vocal parliamentary opposition to the court while devotedly carrying on the king's business in his own county (**29**).

THE ATTITUDE OF THE KING

It has long been customary to blame James I's theories of divine right for the distrust that developed between Crown and parliament during the early seventeenth century. Unlike Elizabeth, who shared his views but preferred to disguise her near-absolutism, James was quite explicit about the theory and practice of kingship. Because he committed his views to paper, historians pluck hopefully at the entrails of his prose to discover his intentions. He is, then, too often judged from his words and not his deeds. His principal works were *The Trew Law of Free Monarchies* (1598), the *Basilikon Doron* (1599), *An Apologie for the Oath of Allegience* (1607), and *A Defence of the Right of Kings against Cardinal Perron* (1615) (**14**). Often quoting his books from memory,

James harangued the House of Commons, comparing himself with God. Kings, like God, have the power 'to make and unmake their subjects. They have the power of raising and casting down, of life and of death, judges over all, and yet accountable to none but God alone'. After the failure of the 1614 parliament, James remarked privately to the Spanish ambassador that 'the House of Commons is a body without a head. The members give their opinions in a disorderly manner. At their meetings nothing is heard but cries, shouts and confusions. I am surprised that my ancestors should ever have allowed such an institution to come into existence' (15, pp. 286-8). Such opinions have received too much attention. Although in 1604 he told the Commons that he could command them 'as an absolute king', James was not, and did not claim to be, absolute in the sense of being free from all restraint. He took his coronation oath – which obliged him to cherish the laws and customs of England – most seriously. He took care always to operate within the Common Law; he never resorted to imprisonment without trial or raised taxes without parliament's consent. He did not practise what he preached. When in 1607 Dr Cowell argued that the king was 'above the law by his absolute power', James repudiated these theories even though they were similar to those used by himself in *The Trew Law* (12). In 1610, when the Commons complained that James was abusing his right to issue proclamations by creating new crimes not recognised by the Common Law, the king consulted his two chief justices and accepted their judgment even though it went against him. A study of two speeches he made to parliament, one in 1610, the other in 1624, will show how 'moderate' and 'constitutional' he could be [doc. 6] (12, p. 48).

The king's belief in divine right was rooted in medieval traditions and was shared by members of the House of Commons (46). James may have lectured parliament on the nature of kingship in order to display his learning; though this is more an explanation of why he made speeches than of the subject matter he chose. He found the doctrine of divine right a useful weapon with which to fight the Commons' attempts to alter the relationship between Crown and parliament to their own advantage. Until the end of the sixteenth century the Commons had played only a very limited part in government. By attempting to demand redress of grievances before supply, by gradually encroaching, mainly through the activity of parliamentary committees, on the day to day work of government, the House of Commons was undermining the prerogative rights of the Crown. While Elizabeth had surrounded her own powers and the rights of parliament with a haze of equivocation, James felt that if encroachments on the prerogative were not challenged the case for the Crown would go by default. He allowed the prerogative to be tested in the courts, a step Elizabeth would never have taken, and he regularly defined his position in speeches to parliament. In 1610, for example, he recalled tartly that in 1604 the Commons had passed the Bill of Assarts, intending to take from him wastelands and woodlands which for centuries had belonged to the Crown. In this and other ways they had 'encroached and crept in upon the king' (**58**, p. 322).

> Put not to me precedents [he warned], unless you will let me reckon precedents too for my prerogative. I would not willingly press you neither would I have you press me. Kings must be trusted, and if you have no trust in my person, why would you propound that to me which was never asked of any king? . . . But be not misled [he concluded], the more wayward you shall be, I shall be the more unwilling to call you to parliament (**58**, p. 324).

The effect of making explicit the traditional rights of the Crown was to widen divisions between king and subject, and raise the fear that 'if the practice should follow the positions, we are not like to leave to our successors that freedom we received from our forefathers' (John Chamberlain). Yet, although James never hid his distaste for parliament, he took pains to deny explicitly any claims to legislate or collect subsidies without it. He pursued no policy of destroying parliament, but was willing to confer with and explain his policies to it. He possibly said too much. By making personal appearances and by sending messages James hoped to guide the Commons. Instead, he irritated them. Probably his greatest mistake was his failure to assert conciliar influence over the Lower House. His greatest fault was a tendency to expand the frontiers of a quarrel with the Commons by raising unnecessary and explosive issues of parliamentary privilege. Forced to justify themselves, the Commons thumbed through collections of medieval precedents to support their claims, and the quarrels, which could have been avoided, turned into serious conflicts involving the very nature of the relationship between Crown and parliament.

THE PARLIAMENT OF 1604-1610

One such conflict marked the opening of the first parliament of the reign. Because he had granted peerages to most of his Council, James was represented in the Commons only by Mr 'Secondary' Herbert and by Sir John Stanhope, mediocrities who allowed Sir Robert Wroth, a veteran parliamentarian, to take the initiative by suggesting an agenda. Six of the seven topics he proposed were eventually discussed by the Commons. The government's case was usually put by Sir Francis Bacon and Sir George More, neither of whom had any official status. The court was therefore eager for a third councillor, Sir John Fortescue, to take his seat as one of the members for Buckinghamshire. Unfortunately Fortescue had only gained his seat after a second election, the first having returned Sir Francis Goodwin, whose candidature was then refused by Chancery on the grounds that he was an outlaw. In March 1604 the Commons reversed this decision and allowed Goodwin to take his seat.

The question at issue — who was to be sole judge of election returns — was one of considerable importance. The precedents were confusing: the Commons had decided disputed election returns until 1406, and Chancery afterwards. Some members felt that if the job were left to Chancery, the government might attempt to pack parliament, not necessarily at the present but at some time in the future. Declaring his indifference as to who was elected, the king told the Commons that he 'had no purpose to impeach their privilege but since they derived all matters of privilege from him and by his grant, he expected they should not be turned against him'. The House responded by arguing that their privileges were their right which no king could ever take away. The dispute ended amicably enough, the Commons agreeing to a new election and James acknowledging the Commons as a court of record and a proper, though not exclusive, judge of election returns. A great deal of time had been wasted on an issue which, with better management, might never have arisen.

In many ways this 1604 session of parliament was a troubled one. Although James had inherited a debt of £400,000 from Elizabeth, and had to pay for her funeral and his own coronation, the Commons declined to grant a subsidy because the four subsidies voted in 1601 were still being collected. The king's plan for 'a perfect union' of England and Scotland met with serious opposition from the Commons. There was trouble, too, over wardship and purveyance, both relics of feudalism which the Tudors had vigorously exploited. 'Purveyance', the right of the royal household to purchase supplies at low prices, provided ample opportunities for profit and abuse. The king's right of 'wardship' of heirs who were minors was probably the biggest grievance of 1604. Although the petition requesting its abolition accepted the need to compensate the Crown and the officers of the Court of Wards for their loss of income, James declined to negotiate, probably because the compensation offered would not fully recompense him for the loss involved. At the end of the session, after James had complained about their attitude to wardship and union with Scotland, the Commons set up a committee of seventy-two members to prepare a statement justifying their behaviour for presentation to the king. Dr Elton has demonstrated that this *Form of Apology and Satisfaction* cannot be regarded as anything more than 'a minority opinion rejected by the House as too extreme' (87, p. 341). Recalling the trouble over election returns, the committee argued that the privileges of parliament had been 'most seriously and dangerously impugned than ever (as we supposed) since the beginning of parliaments'. These privileges were not granted by the king's grace, but were the 'right and due inheritance of every member, no less than their land and goods'. There followed a longwinded justification of the Commons' behaviour; a statement that whereas 'the prerogatives of princes may easily and do daily grow, the privileges of the subject are for the most part at an everlasting stand'; and a list of grievances which they had refrained from pressing on Elizabeth' in regard to her sex and age' (58, pp. 125-40). So intemperate was the tone and language of the Apology that the Commons declined to present it to His Majesty, appointing instead a new committee to revise it. Before this could be done parliament was prorogued and the Apology forever shelved. Too much should not be made of the teething troubles of this first session. The king's implied threats to the privileges of parliament were the result of clumsiness and tactlessness rather than a wish to act despotically. Although he referred sarcastically to 'my masters of the Lower House', in his prerogation speech of 7 July, James became more conciliatory as he grew accustomed to the bellicose ways of the English Commons. They, for the most part, were distrustful of the government, possibly because in Europe generally the powers of kings were increasing, and those of representative assemblies declining. This distrust, however, could be overcome by skilful management and a willingness to redress grievances.

The second session (January-May 1606) turned out to be a happy interlude of fruitful cooperation. Shaken by the discovery of the Gunpowder Plot, king and parliament cooperated in passing harsher penal laws against the Catholics. Two subsidies and four fifteenths (about £250,000) were granted, but not until a list of grievances was ready for presentation to the king. As well as complaining about monopolies, impositions and purveyance, the recent rise in customs duties and the export of iron ordnance, the petition expressed anxiety about such matters as a patent for Green Wax, a dye made of logwood and the making of blue starch. Although James gave a detailed answer (12, pp. 64-9 and p. 55, n.i), nothing could be done to abolish the extraparliamentary taxes so long as the government was crippled with debt. The difficulties of reaching any sort of financial settlement with parliament can be illustrated by examining the protracted negotiations over purveyance which took place during conferences between the Commons and the Lords. Most M.P.s, though not all, agreed that James would have to be compensated for its loss. But how, and to what extent? How could the Commons hold the king to a bargain? How would the money for compensation be raised? Could a levy be distributed fairly, since at present purveyance hit heavily only those areas north of London where the king went hunting? Would compensation take the form of a lump sum or an annual tax? A tax on land, said Yelverton, would prove 'a devil's walk', involving commissions of enquiry to discover exactly how much each man owned and by what right. To those whose title to land was disputable, such a survey was most unpalatable. Predictably, the Commons abandoned the problem of compensation, proceeding instead with a Bill to restrain the excesses of the purveyors. Despite the rejection of this Bill by the Lords, relations between king and Commons remained amicable. By a narrow majority an additional subsidy and two fifteenths were voted; a recognition, perhaps, that the king's demands were justified.

During the third session of 1606-07, James's fondest project, the full political union of England and Scotland was the main subject of debate (111). The king's plan was nothing if not far sighted, and he argued his case well. The two kingdoms would become one, with the same law, religion, and parliament. Free trade would be established, together with the naturalisation of all Scots born after James's accession to the English throne. Despite his determination to have it, union did not come for another hundred years. The Council was apathetic, parliament openly hostile. The behaviour and rewards of those who had come south with James had done nothing to promote sympathy between the two nations. The Scots, said one M.P., were proud, quarrelsome, beggarly and untrustworthy, and had 'not suffered above two kings to die in their beds these two hundred years'. So many difficulties were raised that the king surrendered to English prejudice and abandoned his plans.

THE SESSION OF 1610

In 1610 Salisbury hoped to persuade parliament to pay off the debt of £280,000 (of which £120,000 was an Elizabethan forced loan still to be repaid), and also provide the king with a regular income that would put an end to the annual deficits. He therefore asked for a subsidy of £600,000 to eradicate the debt, improve the navy, and to meet any additional expenses that might arise. His second proposal, a statesmanlike and farreaching fiscal reform, became known as the *Great Contract*.

In return for a permanent grant of £200,000 a year, the king was prepared to negotiate the surrender of wardship and purveyance, and his legal right to debts due to the Crown from the time of Henry VII's reign to Mary's (estimated at £700,000). Circumstances did not favour a speedy settlement. Some M.P.s were reluctant to give money which they felt would be 'wasted and exhausted by the excessive gifts of the king and misgovernance of his officers'. What was the use, asked Wentworth, of drawing 'a silver stream out of the country into the royal cistern if it shall daily run out by private cocks?' (58, p. 262). Past grievances were as burdensome as ever, and there were new complaints to add to the old. Members were indignant about the publication of *The Interpreter* by the Cambridge scholar Dr Cowell, who wrote that the king was 'above the law by his absolute power'. Although James repudiated these ideas and ordered the book's suppression, the affairs probably highlighted, at least for a minority, the dangers of a financially independent monarchy.

While Salisbury negotiated the details of the Great Contract, a Committee of the Whole House spent each afternoon dealing with grievances. On 18 July they presented a massive petition that castigated monopolies, complained of the excessive use of proclamations, asked for the curtailment of the powers of High Commission and the Council of Wales, and demanded that all impositions without parliamentary consent should be 'quite abolished'. They requested also the enforcement of the penal laws, the reinstatement of Puritan clergy silenced in 1604 and some reform of the abuses of pluralism and non-residence. There were complaints, too, against the ecclesiastical courts and against canons not confirmed by parliament (see ch. 6). Running through the petition like a thread of steel is a conviction that the Crown might eventually rule without parliament. It was observed that 'their common and ancient right and liberty [was] much declined and infringed in these late years', and that things which under Elizabeth were practised without offence were now 'more thoroughly scanned by reason of the great mischiefs and inconveniences which the subjects have thereby sustained'. The king's use of proclamations was condemned because they would 'by degrees grow up and increase to the strength and nature of laws . . . and may also in time bring in a new form of arbitrary government upon the realm'. No one denied that the king needed wide powers and a full treasury; no one disbelieved James when he said that he wanted to rule according to the laws and customs of the realm. What worried M.P.s was the possibility that one of James's successors would try to establish absolutism. This fear was clearly expressed during the debate on impositions, the major grievance of the 1610 session. The length and gravity of this discussion leaves no doubt that impositions were feared because they might lead to the decay of parliament. Baron Fleming's judgment in Bate's Case, the Commons told James, could 'be extended much further, even to the utter ruin of the ancient liberty of this kingdom and of your subjects' right of property in their lands and goods' (see p. 28).

Yet, despite their fears, the Commons agreed to the Contract and granted James one subsidy and one fifteenth to relieve his most pressing needs. When, on 23 July, James prorogued parliament until 18 October, he promised to examine carefully their complaints and devise what remedy he could. He had been remarkably patient and conciliatory. In March he answered those who whispered that he planned to alter the constitution and rule as an absolute king [doc. 6]. In May, after banning a debate on impositions, he received a petition claiming as 'an ancient, general and undoubted right of parliament to debate freely all matters which do properly concern the subject and his right or state'. James accepted the petition and allowed the debate to continue, assuring the Commons that he did not plan to meddle with property, nor to impose upon his subjects' lands or goods, but only upon merchandise, and to do that in parliament. He offered to see a dozen members privately, a gesture that moved one anonymous M.P. to write: 'One thing I may not forget which I cannot but with joy remember, to see in what fashion a noble, great, and wise Prince did vouchsafe to speak to his people' (58, p. 331). In July the king promised not to levy any new impositions, and in September he remedied many of the specific complaints against them. At the same time a considerable number of proclamations were withdrawn. Although the Commons were disappointed by what many regarded as a halfhearted response to their complaints, it is difficult to see what more James could have done when so many of the burdens they denounced provided revenues which he could not do without.

During the recess both parties to the Contract reflected on its possible effects. Sir Francis Bacon, who disliked Salisbury and all his works, advised James not to haggle with his subjects like a merchant. Sir Julius Caesar, in a long memorandum, dismissed the Contract as 'a ready passage to a democracy, which is the deadliest enemy to a monarchy'. He argued that the fixed sum of £200,000 a year took no account of future inflation (which did, in fact, slow down considerably during the next decade), and was only £85,000 more than the revenues the king was being asked to surrender. If the Contract were arranged, parliament would be more than ever reluctant to vote subsidies in time of peace. He therefore urged the abandonment of the Contract and the adoption of a policy of retrenchment and reform. There were other, less disinterested critics. Those who profited from the feudal dues to be abolished and officials from the Court of Wards did their best to sabotage the scheme. The merchants, too, rallied to the opposition because they feared that the £200,000 would be raised from trade. Salisbury had dodged the problem of defining exactly how the money would be raised. On reflection, many M.P.s found a permanent land tax or a tax on merchandise equally unpalatable. They also feared that, should James be granted additional revenues, he would dispense altogether with their services. So, when parliament met again in October, both king and Commons raised their price and the Contract collapsed.

The House of Commons were the first to raise the terms. Debating the king's answer to their petition of grievances in a sparsely attended chamber (about 100 members were present on 22 October), Nicholas Fuller suggested that James should abandon impositions as part of the proposed bargain. Dudley Digges, on the other hand, suggested that they should rest content with what had already been offered. There was much talk but no unanimity. Then, on 6 November, the king announced that before he discussed the Contract he wanted compensation for officers of the Court of Wards, and subsidies amounting to £500,000. Although this demand was lower than that of February, the intervening months had revealed that James was asking for the moon. On 8 November negotiations were abandoned. Salisbury continued to struggle for some sort of grant, but the House declined, mounting an attack on the king, for spending 'all upon his favourites and wanton courtiers', that brought a dissolution. The failure of this session was partly the result of distrust and illwill between king and Commons, for a significant number of M.P.s were convinced that 'the good king studied to enthrall the people', intending to free himself from parliament forever. James's reluctance, or inability, to do much about grievances contributed to the distrust. Sir Henry Neville said as much to James himself: between 1604 and 1610 parliament had given four subsidies and seven fifteenths 'which is more than ever was given by any parliament at any time upon any occasion; and yet withal they had no relief of their grievances' (**58**, p. 421).

5 Factions and Favourites

ROBERT CECIL, EARL OF SALISBURY

During the early part of James's reign the conduct of affairs was left largely in the hands of Sir Robert Cecil, created Earl of Salisbury in 1605. Cecil, who had been Secretary of State for nearly ten years, had done more than anyone to secure James's accession, thereby making his own position impregnable. Robert, like his father William Cecil before him, kept a tenacious grip on power, holding at arm's length men of great ability like Sir Francis Bacon, and surrounding himself with creatures of unexceptional talent. Cecil managed affairs with great skill and efficiency, and when in 1608 he assumed the burdens – and profits – of the Treasury, he indeed became 'that great Engin of state, by whom all wheels moved'.

Robert Cecil was a younger son with his fortune to make. His lands, and the great palace he built at Hatfield between 1607 and 1612 at a cost of about £40,000, testify to his success. His profits from office and from suitors anxious to secure his patronage may have gone beyond the acceptable threshold of corruption. Yet at a time when a powerful minister was expected to live in great state, without the benefits of a proper salary, such practices were inevitable. Somewhat illogically, contemporaries distinguished between small benefits and large, and because Cecil's profits from office were so great he was regarded as corrupt. Mrs Prestwich had provided a wealth of evidence to show how Cecil grew rich in the public service, and argues that 'he shared in the profiteering and corruption which penetrated the interstices of government to a degree far beyond that of Elizabeth's reign' (59, p. 47). Her harsh and detailed criticisms are new; Cecil has usually been credited with statesmanship and a modest show of reforming zeal (40, 108). There is no simple answer to the problem of whether or not this complex and devious politician was corrupt: as Professor Hurstfield has pointed out, in a spirited review of Mrs Prestwich's biography of Cranfield, questions of political morality in seventeenth-century England cannot be judged by 'the twentieth-century standards of a western European state' (95). As an administrator, Cecil had served a long apprenticeship under his father Lord Burghley, an experience that made it difficult for him to cope with the changed political circumstances of James's reign. Allowing for his great service in securing a peaceful succession, it seems fair to indict Cecil with having done little to help James to settle in his new kingdom. If James had been better advised and served in the years immediately after 1603 it is probable that some difficulties of the early years might have been avoided. The development, for instance, of a king's party in the Commons would have made the government's task easier; but Cecil took little trouble with parliament. Jealous of Francis Bacon, he neglected to use him to lead the Commons, preferring instead to manage affairs by a far from satisfactory use of conferences between the two Houses. An assessment of the financial situation, together with warnings of the dangers of extravagance, might have discouraged James from spending so freely. But so anxious was Cecil to ingratiate himself with his new master, that he avoided such action. No cloud was allowed to overshadow the king's accession. When the Archbishop of York dared to criticize the king's extravagance he was denounced by Cecil, who possibly felt nervous of curbing royal spending when he was taking so much himself. Later, when money was scarcer, he did remonstrate gently with James; but by then the king was set in his extravagant ways.

Although Cecil refused to advance able administrators, one of whom might acquire the practical experience to be his successor, he was prepared to embark on some cautious reforms. A finely developed instinct for survival prevented him from launching a programme of retrenchment and reform at court, but he carried through some drastic reforms of the Court of Wards and devised a constructive plan to improve finances by means of the *Great Contract* with parliament (p. 42). He was prepared to risk his health and his standing with the king in an attempt to carry through this long overdue fiscal reform. Ironically, his increase of impositions in 1608 which Sir Julius Caesar accurately forecast would 'prove the most gainful to the king and his posterity of any one day's work by any Lord Treasurer since the time of King Edward III', contributed to the Contract's failure. Salisbury's slack administration, his introduction of impositions, the farming of customs, the abuses and extravagance of the court, were all criticised by the Commons, and the Contract collapsed. So although a full assessment of Cecil's career must await Professor Hurstfield's forthcoming biography, it is difficult not to agree with Francis Bacon's unkind epitaph, when he remarked to James: 'I do think he was no fit counsellor to make your affairs better, but yet he was fit to have kept them from getting worse.'

THE HOWARDS

During the first decade of the reign Salisbury channelled offices, power and wealth to a number of supporters, great and small. In consequence, the Cecilian faction dominated politics until the minister's death in 1612. Factional struggle was the accepted method of opposition in the early seventeenth century, an inevitable accompaniment of personal monarchy. Factional groupings gathered round rival councillors, who consolidated their positions by dispensing patronage and promising favours. Elizabeth had skilfully balanced one faction against another. 'The principal note of her reign', remarked Naunton, 'will be that she ruled much by faction and parties, which she herself both made, upheld and weakened as her own judgement advised.' In 1601 she temporarily lost her grip on the Earl of Essex who, jealous of Cecil's influence, tried forcibly to seize control, paying for failure with his life. The Main Plot of 1603 was the last attempt of Cecil's enemies to unseat him; thereafter he was supreme. Elizabeth had been reluctant to give the Cecils a monopoly of power. When Burleigh died, it was the Earl of Dorset, not Robert Cecil, who succeeded him as Treasurer. Although Robert was allowed to succeed his father as Master of the Wards, Elizabeth took from him the Chancellorship of the Duchy of Lancaster. James showed no such care, concentrating most available favours on Cecil and the Howard family, who ached for the positions of power and profit denied them by Elizabeth. Their leader was Henry Howard, Earl of Northampton, the impoverished younger brother of the Duke of Norfolk executed for treason in 1572. Northampton was shallow, malicious, and a skilful intriguer who had joined with Cecil to poison James's mind against Sir Walter Raleigh and Lord Cobham, thereby eliminating some of his rivals at court. His circle included his nephew, the Earl of Suffolk and his grandson, the Earl of Arundel, as well as Lord Knollys and the Earl of Nottingham, Lord Admiral of England. Intoxicated by the unaccustomed warmth of royal favour, the Howards at first were content to share the pickings with Salisbury, the Scots and the Earl of Dorset, nicknamed Lord Fill-Sack because of the money he was taking from the Treasury. By family tradition the Howards were crypto-Catholics. As the reign advanced they began to favour a Spanish alliance, a relaxation of the penal laws against Catholics and – for obvious reasons – the avoidance of encounters with parliament. In 1613 their influence was strengthened by the arrival from Madrid of possibly the most able diplomats in Europe, ambassador Sarmiento, later Count Gondomar. The Howards were opposed by a faction which included Archbishop Abbot, the Earls of Pembroke, Southampton and Montgomery, Sir Henry Neville, Sir Ralph Winwood and Sir Thomas

Overbury. Broadly speaking, they stood for a 'Protestant', anti-Spanish foreign policy, the enforcement of the penal laws, financial reform and cooperation with parliament (**50**).

Both factions quivered with apprehension when the first of the great Jacobean favourites appeared. Various male beauties, such as Lord Hay, had already caught the king's eye, but none had risen to pre-eminence. Scandalmongers tell how the Countess of Suffolk showed solicitude for the king, and for her own family, when she 'did look out choice young men whom she daily curled, and perfumed their breaths'. The man who took the king's fancy in 1607, however, had no connection with the Howards. Just over twenty-one years old, handsome, tall and athletic, Robert Carr was a Scot who had come south with James in 1603, receiving no attention until he fell from his horse in the tiltyard. The king supervised his convalescence and taught him Latin. Soon James was leaning on his arm and 'smoothing his ruffled garment', telling his Council that 'he did take more delight in his company and conversation than in any man's living'. Carr received from James money and land in abundance and in 1611 was created Viscount Rochester. The pigeon-brained favourite leaned heavily on his friend, an accomplished Gloucestershire gentleman called Sir Thomas Overbury. Here lay the cause of Howard's apprehension, for Overbury — according to Bishop Goodman — was 'truly very insolent, and one who did much abuse the family of the Howards'. At court he was associated with the anti-Spanish faction.

All was set in flux when Salisbury died in 1612. The Howards desired the Treasury, the Secretaryship and control of the Court of Wards, but feared that Overbury and Carr would thwart them. As each faction pressed for an advantage, wagers flew 'up and down as thick and as variable as if it were a cockpit' (Chamberlain). For a time, James resisted all pressure. Sir George Carew, a man independent of either faction, was given the Court of Wards, and when Carew died at the end of the year, it went to Sir Walter Cope. Commissioners were put in charge of the Treasury, while the king himself undertook the duties of Secretary. Perhaps he remembered his great days in Scotland and hoped to repeat that triumph in England, but he lacked the energy to make the experiment a success. In 1614 Sir Ralph Winwood was appointed Secretary and the factions were balanced by making Suffolk Treasurer.

So, for the moment, neither faction triumphed. The Howards then enjoyed a marvellous stroke of luck. The favourite became enchanted by Lady Frances Howard, the Earl of Suffolk's daughter, already inconveniently married to the Earl of Essex. Never dreaming that the affair would lead to marriage, Overbury helped with the seduction of Lady Frances, whose family decided to seek an annulment on the grounds of her husband's alleged impotency. The inevitable opposition from the anti-Spanish faction was neatly outflanked, while Overbury was confined to the tower for refusing the king's offer of a diplomatic post abroad [**doc. 7**]. He died there, mysteriously, in September 1613.

THE PARLIAMENT OF 1614

The Howards' triumph was brief but, while it lasted, effective. The struggle of the factions now spilled over into parliament, which was called in 1614 to help fill the empty treasury and pay off the debt of £680,000. Preparations for the session were feebly conceived and incompetently executed. Following Tudor practice, a modest attempt was made to secure the return of a few members sympathetic to the court, who might anchor the unaligned gentry firmly to the Crown. When parliament met, rumour so exaggerated the government's activities that the Commons were enraged by what they chose to regard as excessive and improper meddling in elections, elections which were, in fact, perfectly normal (**55**). Although nearly one-third of the Commons, possibly 135 out of 464, had some connection with the court, this parliament proved to be more turbulent than any other during the reign of James. There was trouble over what James later called 'a strange beast called undertakers'. Sir Henry Neville, a friend of the favourite and of the Earl of Southampton, a man on easy terms with many of the more radical members of parliament, put forward 'certain propositions' which he hoped would promote goodwill between king and Commons. He suggested that if concessions were made to the Crown's critics in the Commons, 'he dared undertake for most of them that the king's majesty, proceeding in a gracious course towards his people, should find these gentlemen exceeding willing to do him service'. Neville recommended a clearer definition of the treason laws, the repeal of 'obsolete and snarling laws' and some relaxation of purveyance: all very sensible but hardly spectacular. Sir Francis Bacon also urged concessions and proposed that the Council should influence elections at 'the Boroughs of the Cinque Ports, and of the Duchy, and other boroughs at the devotion of diverse [of] the king's councillors, for the placing [of] persons well affected and discreet'. He also wondered what weapons could be used against 'the popular party' in the Commons, 'for the securing of them, intimidating of them or holding them in hopes ... whereby they may be dissolved, or weakened, or won'. He decided that patronage would do the trick. But Bacon's scheme was not implemented, while neither he nor Neville had any remedy for impositions, monopolies or ecclesiastical abuses, all of obsessive concern to many in the Commons.

The government's preparations, leaked deliberately by courtiers who wanted this parliament to fail, caused the sort of trouble they were designed to prevent. Neville's propositions and Bacon's scheme for electoral management were disfigured by gossip into a plot to sweeten the Commons by crude bargaining and corrupt electioneering. Rumours of undertaking were investigated by a committee, which condemned the practice without proving that it had taken place, precipitating a chorus of condemnation from the House. Eventually the tumult subsided, but not before Sir Thomas Parry, Chancellor of the Duchy of Lancaster, had been expelled for interfering with the election at Stockbridge. This was the only case the committee could produce, and it made the most of it. Historians have been no more successful in discovering evidence of sharp practice. Unfounded or not, the rumours shattered the government's prestige, wasted valuable time, and put the Commons in an ugly mood. Hopes of a swift supply were dashed to the ground. When Secretary Winwood suggested an immediate grant he received little support even from his colleagues, and none at all from the rest of the House.

Instead of debating supply the Commons discussed impositions. The king, they were told, had no intention of surrendering to agitation. His study of precedents and the advice of his ministers and judges, convinced him that the abolition of impositions would diminish his prerogative. Nothing, however, that the councillors said could divert the flood of criticism, which surged more strongly when Bishop Neile accused the Commons of sedition for refusing a conference with the Lords. The Lower House at once abandoned all thought of proceeding with the king's business and instead devoted its considerable energies to hunting the bishop. From 21 May until 3 June they occupied themselves with this lively but fruitless affair. The courtiers' attempts to regain control resembled attempts to catch smoke with a butterfly net. Ignoring a warning from James, the House careered on its way towards the threatened dissolution. Perhaps with the Great Contract in mind, they informed the king of their willingness to grant supply if he would cancel impositions; but James refused to haggle. The end came, as in 1610, when the favourites were attacked. Christopher Neville called them 'spaniels to the King and wolves to the people'; while John Hoskyns, who was in the pay of the Earl of Northampton, cried out that 'wise princes put away strangers as Canute, when he meant to plant himself here, sent back his Danes'. When he hinted at a violent final solution to the curse of the Scottish favourites, parliament was dissolved.

The 1614 parliament, having sat for two months without passing a single measure, was soon called the 'Addled Parliament'. Rumours of undertaking had produced an inflammatory atmosphere which made the task of management impossible. The leader of the four Councillors in the House was Sir Ralph Winwood, appointed Secretary of State only seven days before the session opened. He had never before sat in parliament. Opposed by the Howards, his efforts were impeded by disappointed contenders for the Secretaryship like Herbert, Lake and Caesar. Another key figure, Ranulf Crew, had not sat in parliament since 1597 and had lost whatever touch he once possessed. More formidable personalities like Bacon, Yelverton, Caesar, Neville and Wotton were often strangely silent at crucial moments, or else differed publicly. The failure of management, however, is not sufficient explanation of the confusion that occurred. Experienced opponents of the court, like Sir Edwin Sandys, were no more successful than officials at harnessing the energies or checking the turbulence of M.P.s. Strong feeling against impositions produced ugly scenes and a determination to refuse supply until the king listened to their complaints. As in 1610, the Commons questioned James's right to impositions, fearing that such revenue would lay secure foundations for absolutism.

Yet after making allowance for the grievances of the Commons and the weakness of officials, it is difficult to avoid the conclusion that the disaster of 1614 was caused largely by courtly Luddites out to cripple the parliamentary machine. The Spanish faction had been opposed to this parliament right from the start and, once it met, worked hard to wreck it. Sir Samuel Sandys believed that 'more bones' had 'been cast into this parliament to divert the good proceedings of the House, than in all the parliaments I have known'. Information about Neville's propositions was deliberately leaked and the row about undertaking artificially fostered (**55**, ch. 10). Chamberlain reported that after the dissolution 'upon examination it fell out there was a plot discovered to overthrow all orderly proceedings in this parliament, and to make it utterly void, by insisting upon dangerous points as taking away impositions, restoring of silenced ministers, and removing the Scots, with other matters likely to make the king lose all patience'. An enquiry established that Sir Charles Cornwallis, a client of Northampton had paid Hoskyns £20 to make trouble in the Commons. Hoskyns did his job well. Having demanded that discussion of impositions should precede supply, he had gone on to denounce High Commission and verbally to assault the favourites so savagely that James hastened to rid himself of his tormentors by dissolving parliament (**3**, i, 540).

Shortly afterwards James complained to the Spanish ambassador that the House of Commons was a body without a head, its members working in great disorder and confusion. He expressed astonishment that his predecessors had tolerated such an assembly. After the dissolution, those who had denied the king's right to levy impositions were summoned to Whitehall to watch their notes being burnt, while James peeped from behind a curtain. Financial disaster was avoided by the collection of a free gift from courtiers and London merchants, and by the launching of a benevolence, its passage eased by a proclamation granting many of the bills of grace with which James had vainly tried to woo parliament. The money raised by such means amounted to little more than £66,000. Living from day to day, selling titles of honour and borrowing from anyone who would lend, the government managed to conduct affairs without plunging into a financial crisis. Despite rumours of a new parliament, it was seven years before another met.

BUCKINGHAM

The dissolution seemed a vindication of the Howards' attitude to parliament and should have consolidated their position. But Northampton died suddenly within a week of parliament's end, while the anti-Spanish faction produced a trump card in the person of George Villiers, an exceptionally beautiful young man who appeared at court in 1614. A syndicate of sponsors, including the queen and the Archbishop of Canterbury, set about manoeuvring him into a position where he could supplant Carr (now Earl of Somerset) in the king's affections. 'We could have no way so good to effectuate that which was the common desire, as to bring in another in his room', wrote the Primate of All England. In September 1615, Abbot's faction struck again by carrying to James a report that Overbury had been murdered during his imprisonment in the tower two years before. The king at once ordered an investigation, insisting that justice be done however much dirty linen was exposed. There was a great deal: adultery, witchcraft, perjury and murder (75). Lady Somerset pleaded guilty, though her husband protested his innocence till the end. Both were sentenced to death and then reprieved, remaining in prison until 1622, when they were released on condition that they lived quietly in the country [docs. 8, 9]. The Howards did not immediately fall. Nottingham clung to the Admiralty until 1618 when, at the age of eighty he resigned, after an enquiry had exposed the malpractices of his stewardship. Meanwhile, the anti-Spanish faction had been pushing through a programme of financial and administrative reform which exposed the epic embezzlement of Suffolk at the Treasury. It was found that the 'Earl, Countess and Sir John Bingley have divers times taken great sums of money out of His Majesty's Treasure and employed the same about their own or other private uses'. Suffolk was sacked and, together with his wife, fined and imprisoned. James, who was ever tender to the mighty when they fell, ordered their release and had their fine reduced. Ironically, the fall of the Howards did little for the anti-Spanish faction. James did not adopt their policies. Parliament was not recalled and the king continued to look favourably in the direction of Madrid. George Villiers, who had been groomed to counterbalance the influence of the Howards, proved to have a mind of his own.

Villiers was the younger son by a second marriage of a Leicestershire knight. Bishop Goodman described him as 'the handsomest bodied man in England', while John Hacket wrote that 'from the sole of his foot to the crown of his head there was no blemish in him'. His rise was extraordinarily rapid. In 1616 he became Master of the Horse, a Knight of the Garter and Viscount Villiers. In the following year he was made Earl of Buckingham and in 1618, Marquis. In 1623 he became a Duke. The king was infatuated with him. When he conferred the earldom on Villiers in 1617 he told the Council that

> I, James, am neither God nor an angel, but a man like any other. Therefore I act like a man, and confess to loving those dear to me more than other men. You may be sure that I love the Earl of Buckingham more than anyone else, and more than you who are here assembled. I wish to speak in my own behalf, and not to have it thought to be a defect. Christ has his John, and I have my George.

It was a statement as extraordinary for its candour as its blasphemy.

Buckingham was not without ability. He was content, until 1623, to follow the king's policies and was prepared to cooperate with parliament. In his heart he shared the prejudice of the English country gentlemen against Spain. He had the sense to take advice and to make use of the reforming zeal of able men like Francis Bacon and Lionel Cranfield. Thus the early years of his ascendancy were characterised by an attempt to reform the administration and improve the finances (**59**). By 1621 Buckingham had acquired an almost complete monopoly of patronage and royal favour. He could 'open the Sluice of Honours to whom, and shut it against whom he pleased'. The kindred of the favourite shared his good fortune. So successful was his mother in advancing the interests of her friends that the Spanish ambassador observed that England was ripe for conversion to Catholicism, since more people worshipped the mother than the son. Buckingham's two brothers, Christopher and John, the former a congenital idiot, received pensions, earldoms and offices, while remoter kin basked in his reflected glory. At the end of his life James became increasingly dependent upon the Villiers family. Queen Anne and Prince Henry were dead, the Princess Elizabeth in Germany; only Prince Charles remained, and he was shy and withdrawn. The king therefore turned to Buckingham and his family for the attention and affection he needed to receive and bestow. He played the role of grandfather to Buckingham's children. Writing to his 'sweet boys' when they were away in Madrid, James told the Duke: 'Kate and thy sister supped with me on Saturday night last and yesterday both dined and supped with me, and so shall do still with God's grace, as long as I am here; and little grandchild with her four teeth is, God be thanked, well weaned.'

As Buckingham grew more confident of James's dependence on him so he began to assert himself. He bullied the old king into allowing Charles and himself to visit Spain in 1623 and, on returning, allied with the opposition in parliament to force his own foreign policy on the king. There is no good biography of Buckingham that carefully assesses his influence over James. It seems likely, on a careful reading of Chamberlain and other contemporary observers of the court, that James retained an independence of judgment greater than has long been supposed. Dr Ruigh's study of the 1624 parliament confirms this impression (**61**). Although the Duke coerced James into abandoning able servants like Cranfield and the Earl of Bristol because they had opposed his will, he failed to obtain from James a declaration of war against Spain, the king managing to direct the attack against Germany instead (p. 91). This was a difficult and dangerous time for Buckingham, for although his faction was supreme the 'Spanish Party' still existed. The Earl of Arundel, Sir George Calvert and Sir Richard Weston favoured the alliance with Spain, while out of loyalty to James, as well as for reasons of state, important officials like Lord Keeper Williams, Lord Treasurer Cranfield and the Earl of Bristol, ambassador in Madrid, opposed the favourite's scheme. Most dangerous of all Buckingham's adversaries was the Earl of Pembroke, whose desire to be rid of the Duke was evenly matched by his desire to fight Spain. In handling the conspiracies against him Buckingham displayed great political sagacity (**61**). He managed to retain the affection of both the old king and the new, 'conferring all the honours and all the offices of the three kingdoms, without a rival; in dispensing whereof he was guided more by the rules of appetite than of judgement' (**4**, i, 12).

6   The Jacobean Church

JAMES AND THE PURITANS

By 1603 the Church of England was well established; only men over fifty could recall a time before the Elizabethan settlement of 1559. Abuses attacked then and during the Reformation Parliament seemed as pernicious as ever. At the root of most problems was the poverty of the Church. Because so much Church property had passed into lay hands, many ministers had to serve more than one parish if they were to earn a decent living. Thus pluralism and non-residence, and the ignorance of many of the clergy, were probably the worst evils. James I put an end to the unmerciful plundering of the Church that had gone on during Elizabeth's reign. He forbad his bishops to part with any property belonging to their sees and was prompt in filling vacancies – unlike Elizabeth, who had often kept sees vacant so as to pocket episcopal revenues. He also refused to take money for appointments to ecclesiastical offices [**doc. 10**]. Whereas James hoped to remedy clerical poverty by putting an end to lay despoliation of the Church, radical Puritan reformers wanted to confiscate the remaining property of bishops, deans and chapters and redistribute this wealth among the lower clergy. The king refused to contemplate such action and backed his bishops against their Puritan critics.

In discussing James and the Puritans we are at once up against the problem of definition (**53**, ch. 2). Puritanism was born of discontent with the Elizabethan settlement, and the queen's refusal to consider any further reformation. It is a vague term whose meaning changed as the years passed. Although Puritanism often attracted persons of a radical and censorious temperament, its revolutionary phase, during which the radicals tried to impose a Presbyterian organisation on the national Church, was shortlived. Harassed by Star Chamber and High Commission, Puritan nonconformity was reduced to a shadow. By 1593 the Puritan movement was dead. What survived was a way of life and an attitude of mind, dedicated to moderate reforms that would make the Church more protestant. Jacobean Puritans, then, are Englishmen who disliked Sabbath breaking, church ales and stage plays, and who wished to purify the Church of England of popery in order to bring it into line with the best reformed churches on the continent. Although many of them quarrelled with the bishops, not all were opposed to episcopacy in principle. Following contemporary usage, the Separatists are excluded, for Puritans were regarded as members of the Church of England committed to reforming it from within (92). They enjoyed the support of many members of the laity, either because such persons genuinely sympathised with the Puritan programme of reform, or because they saw in such agitation a means of satisfying anticlerical ambitions: the hope of a further secularisation of ecclesiastical endowments and the hope of emancipation form the moral discipline exercised by the church courts. Although Puritans were found among all sorts and conditions of men, an influential minority came from the ranks of the nobility and gentry. A much larger number, who were more inclined to be radical, came from what seventeenth-century Englishmen called 'the middling sort of people', most of them tradesmen, clothiers and freeholders (42, 44).

Because the definition of a Puritan adopted here is broad and rather vague, we must beware of using it merely as another word for 'Protestant'. The difficulties of trying to distinguish between Puritan and non-Puritan are tremendous (90). Puritans were anxious to purify and reform the Church. Yet there were many people in Jacobean England, including the king and his bishops, who genuinely wanted to reform abuses and improve standards of clerical education and behaviour, who cannot in any way be regarded as Puritans. A recent study of lectureships, long held to be a Puritan device for recruiting and financing a preaching ministry, has shown that they were never an exclusively Puritan preserve, not even in London where the radicals were stronger than elsewhere (63). A passion for sermons and a determination to exercise control over the clergy were not, after all, Puritan monopolies. An emphasis on the strict observance of Sunday was another characteristic of Puritanism; but this too was not restricted to Puritans. Whether or not there were theological differences between Puritans and non-Puritans is a matter of dispute. Mr John New, in his book *Anglican and Puritan: The basis of their opposition*, tried to show that the two parties were divided by irreconcilable theologies (57). Charles and Catherine George, in a more persuasive book *The Protestant Mind of the English Reformation*, concluded: 'In our effort to find a distinguishing line between "Puritan" and Anglican, we have found no issue, doctrinal or ecclesiastical, of which we can speak in other than relative terms. The so-called "Puritans" never either monopolize the concept or viewpoint in question or universally exhibit it' (37, p. 405). They observe that 'the "Puritan" thinks of himself as simply more

57

intensely religious, Christian, and Protestant (and specifically more English Protestant) than the ordinary churchgoer, and especially more than those who oppose him' (**37**, p. 397).

Any estimate of the number of Puritans in England in 1603 will obviously reflect the definition chosen. R. G. Usher estimated the number of Puritan ministers as 281 out of a total of about 9,000, a figure many historians reject because they think his definition of a Puritan too narrow (**69**). The number of Puritan laymen is probably impossible to assess. Any numerical weakness was compensated by a remarkably effective organisation, which was used in 1603 to canvass support for a petition that was presented to King James. The demands were studiously moderate. James was asked to place restrictions on pluralism and non-residence and to increase the stipends of preaching ministers. The petition asked also for the surplice 'not to be urged' and the *ex officio* oath to be 'more sparingly used'. Other requests included the abolition of the use of the sign of the cross in baptism, the removal of such terms as 'priest' and 'absolution' from the Prayer Book, greater uniformity of doctrine and some participation, reconcilable with episcopal authority, of the lower clergy in ordination and discipline (**53**, ch. 12). The king was not unsympathetic to the Puritans and their Millenary Petition. A Calvinist accustomed to the dour simplicities of the Presbyterian Church of Scotland, James had already indicated to a deputation of Scottish ministers that he would 'show favour to honest men, but not to Anabaptists. In the preface to the English edition of *Basilikon Doron* he announced that 'the name of Puritan . . . doth properly belong to that vile sect amongst the Anabaptists called the Family of Love' and to the few 'brain-sick and heady preachers', like Browne and Penry, who had 'contempt for the civil magistrate'. For those godly preachers who felt that 'their bishops smell of a papal supremacy' and who regarded Prayer Book ceremonies as 'outward badges of popish errors', James professed respect: 'I do equally love and honour the learned and grave men of either of these opinions. It can no way become me to pronounce so lightly a sentence in so old a controversy' (**10**, p. 144). In the light of such opinions, the Archbishop of Canterbury and his colleagues were troubled by the possibility of the concessions James might make, and pleaded that a church that had stood for forty years should be left untouched. To this the king replied: 'It was no reason that because a man had been sick of the pox forty years, therefore he should not be cured at length!'

Ignoring episcopal opposition, the king met the moderate spokesman of the Puritans at Hampton Court in January 1604. When it came to writing the official account of the Conference, William Barlow, Bishop of Rochester, created an impression that James and the bishops had stood united against a Puritan onslaught. Thinking that the Puritans wanted a Presbyterian system, the king lost his temper, screeched 'no bishop, no king', and threatened that if the Puritans refused to conform he would 'harry them out of the land'. Dr Curtis has raised serious doubts about this traditional view that the conference was a failure for which James was primarily responsible (85). The king echoed many of the criticisms of the Puritans. Genuinely anxious to strengthen the unity of the Church, he was prepared to join them in reforming proved abuses and removing errors. Only once, when Reynolds used the word *presbyter*, did the king become angry. The conference ended amicably. James had agreed about the need to eliminate pluralism, improve the quality of the ministers and to establish a preaching ministry. High Commission was to be reformed. In ordaining, suspending, degrading and depriving ministers, bishops were to be assisted by other ministers. If, in the long term, the conference was regarded as a failure, this was because the bishops were able to block most of the agreed reforms. The only lasting changes were a number of small reforms which found their way into the Prayer Book and the Canons of 1604, and the publication of one uniform translation of the Bible, the Authorised Version of 1611.

By stressing the moderation of the Millenary Petition it is possible to indict James and his bishops with having failed to devise a lasting compromise with the Puritans. It is, however, arguable that James well understood what lay behind this moderation, and how necessary it was to give the Puritans an opportunity of revealing their true ends. The 'moderate' demands would then be seen to be but the thin end of a wedge. The request that 'discipline and excommunication may be administered according to Christ's own institution', and that no man be excommunicated 'without the consent of his pastor' would, if granted, have radically changed the government of the Church. Moderate spokesmen like Reynolds received instructions from a conclave of delegates which included many radicals who had organised a campaign of support reminiscent of the Presbyterian agitation of the 1580s (32). Not surprisingly, it was the radicals who were most disappointed by the results of Hampton Court, while the moderates decided to conform.

It is probable that the mildness of the Puritan spokesmen in 1604 persuaded James that few clergymen would make an open stand against outward conformity. The king made a distinction between the godly and the subversive Puritan. While the lapses of the former could be tolerated, the opinions of the latter could not, for they threatened the basis of government in both Church and State. In 1604 new Canons were drawn up by Convocation in an attempt to define the laws and beliefs of the Church and to establish whether the Puritans were, as Bancroft put it, 'either joined with them or severed from them'. Canon XXXV required that candidates for holy orders and all unbeneficed ministers must subscribe to three articles, acknowledging the royal supremacy and affirming that neither the Prayer Book nor the Thirty-nine Articles were contrary to the word of God. It was therefore with a heavy armoury that Bancroft began the drive for conformity. Very few Puritans were unable to accept the royal supremacy, but most found it difficult to accept that the Prayer Book and the Articles were agreeable to the word of God. James, however, had commanded the bishops at Hampton Court to treat the Puritans gently. In a proclamation of 16 July 1604 he again required them 'by conferences, arguments, persuasions and by all other ways of love and gentleness, to reclaim all that be in the ministry to obedience to our church laws . . . [so that the] . . . uniformity which we desire may be wrought by clemency and by weight of reason, and not by rigour of law' (**12**, p. 137).

Bancroft instructed the bishops to distinguish between the Puritan who 'promiseth conformity, but is as yet unwilling to subscribe' and he that 'in his obstinacy will be induced to yield to neither'. The former sort were not required to subscribe in the hope that they would eventually be won over (**28**). In the dioceses there were many bishops who did not demand subscription and some who did not even enforce conformity. In the diocese of York, for example, while Toby Mathew was Archbishop (1606-28), numerous clergy whose consciences jibbed at conformity were allowed to go in peace (**49**). Thus the Church was purged only of its most uncompromising ministers who refused both conformity and subscription. Contemporaries claimed that there were 300 'silenced ministers' but Dr Babbage has cut this estimate down to 150, of whom not more than 90 were deprived of their benefices (**28**, ch. 6). Some eminent Puritans were treated very leniently and others overcame their difficulties of conscience by arranging for a curate to perform those ceremonies which they could not stomach. Only the most inflexible were compelled to pursue their ministries abroad, in Leyden and Amsterdam, and later in America. To preserve the unity of the Church and to prevent the disaster of separatism, both James and the Puritans had agreed to tolerate a measure of difference and disagreement. By combining firmness with a refusal to insist on absolute conformity, the king successfully isolated the subversive Puritans from the majority of their colleagues, thereby containing and controlling the non-conformist tradition in the Church which by now was over forty years old.

THE BISHOPS AND THEIR PROBLEMS

The Jacobean bishops are surrounded by imputations of scandal that persist however often they are refuted. Professor Trevor-Roper has described them as 'worldly, courtly, talented, place-hunting *dilettanti*, the ornamental betrayers of the church', who took their character as well as their name from the king they were appointed to serve (110). The activities of the bishops of Bath and Wells during this period have confirmed the Professor's strictures in at least one diocese (39). There is need for a thorough study of the bishops as a group: the admittedly inadequate work that has been done suggests that although there were time-servers among them, the majority were learned and diligent diocesans (99). As such they compare not unfavourably with their predecessors, some of whom were scandalous to a degree greater than most Jacobeans. Several Elizabethan bishops, notably Sandys of York and Barlow of St Davids, were nepotists on a grand scale, and others such as Cheney of Gloucester were very negligent. Only a few were scholars of any repute, in great contrast to the Jacobeans. Since the bishops, as well as being churchmen, were involved in politics they had to spend a lot of time at court. Because their duties involved licensing books, preaching obedience to the Crown, meeting in parliament and working as civil servants, James kept a rigorous control over appointments. Ability, administrative skill and considerable education were essential for preferment. Only nine out of the forty men elevated by James were not scholars. Twenty-seven of them had received a thorough grounding in ecclesiastical administration by serving as deans (98).

James's appointments display a characteristic emphasis on moderation, for the majority were Calvinists who were careful not to disturb the peace of the Church by enforcing the canons too rigorously. Four outstanding bishops – Lancelot Andrews of Winchester, Richard Neile of Durham, John Buckeridge of Rochester and Samuel Harsnett of Chichester – were leaders of a small group of clergymen, later called *Arminians*, who emphasised the sacramental and liturgical aspects of worship and who favoured a modification of Calvinist doctrines such as predestination. These appointments, perhaps, were ill-considered, though there were not enough of them to threaten the theological unanimity of the Church's leadership. The reintroduction of ceremonies widely regarded as popish, and the Arminian insistence that episcopacy was divinely ordained, helped to revive Puritan agitation which James had done so much to contain. Yet this did not occur until the next reign when circumstances were very different. James's refusal to promote William Laud, despite Buckingham's protestations on his behalf, suggests that the king was conscious of the danger.

Probably the only way in which one can generalize about the Jacobean bishops is from the manner of their appointment. It is in this sense only that the bishops reflect the nature of the secular government, which operated on foundations of gigantic jobbery. Promotion in the Church, as well as in the State, required a patron, so that toadying and string-pulling were as normal as breathing. Actual instances are sometimes quoted with horror. The Bishop of Llandaff, the occupant of a poverty-stricken see, wrote to Buckingham saying: 'My Lord, I am grown an old man, and am like old household stuff, apt to be broke upon oft removing. I desire it, therefore, but once and for all, be it Ely or Bath and Wells, and I will spend the remainder of my days in writing a history of your good deeds to me and others, wherein I may vindicate you from the obloquy of this present wicked age' (**110**, p. 138). Given the system of patronage without which preferment was impossible, such a letter is not as scandalous as might at first appear. This was the conventional approach; it was no use promising to be a good shepherd of the flock. In any case, it does not seem as if Buckingham's influence on ecclesiastical preferment after 1616 produced a particularly bad crop of bishops. The king continued, until the end, to exercise a careful control over appointments (**98**).

The patronage system was reinforced by the poverty of many bishops. As wealthier sees became available, the higher clergy would jostle excitedly for preferment and prod their patrons to put in a good word with the king. It was need of money, usually a genuine need, that set the bishops 'posting and suing' whenever a see became vacant, 'so sharp set men are nowadays for every little profit of preferment' (**3**, ii, 375). It is not surprising that hypocrites and timeservers managed to scramble on to the episcopal bench. Among the worldly and negligent were men like John Williams, a devious politician who spent over twenty years as Bishop of Lincoln before he visited his diocese; and Bishop Bayley of Bangor, who is chiefly remembered for blasphemously drinking a toast to a fellow bishop with the words 'Ely, Ely, Lama Sabacthani'. Thornborough of Worcester seems to have devoted most of his attention to establishing his relatives in his diocese and to quarrelling with his Dean and Chapter, who wanted to stop him storing hay in the cathedral chapel. Because some were disreputable, eventually all were condemned. Yet most of the bishops were learned, pious and conscientious men.

'The world wanted learning to know how learned this man was', wrote Thomas Fuller, of Lancelot Andrewes. One of the translators of the Authorised Version, the Bishop of Winchester would have been an ornament to the Church in any age. Another translator of the Bible was Nicholas Felton, a Cambridge scholar who was made Bishop of Ely in 1619 and who thereafter devoted himself to the care of his diocese, where he was noted for his preaching, goodness and charity. Two other important scholars who helped with the Authorised Version were Miles Smith and John Overall. Smith, who prepared the final draft for publication, was made Bishop of Gloucester. Overall became Bishop of Coventry and Lichfield in 1614 and was translated to Norwich four years later, where he was remembered as 'a discreet presser of conformity' (Fuller). A much stricter bishop, described by Prynne as a 'furious Hildebrand', was Samual Harsnet, an Arminian who was successively Bishop of Chichester and then Norwich. Another conscientious diocesan was George Carleton, Bishop of Chichester, a distinguished scholar who had been the king's principal representative at the Synod of Dort, convened by the Dutch in 1619 to condemn Arminian theology. Three other bishops of energy and ability were John King of London, Richard Neile of Durham and John Davenant of Salisbury. The northern province was under the care of Toby Mathew, an Elizabethan bishop elevated to York by James I. 'He died yearly in report', says Fuller, referring to rumours of the old man's death which regularly circulated around London, rumours it was said, which were started by Mathew himself. 'I doubt not', continues Fuller, 'but that in the Apostle's sense he died daily in his mortifying meditations.' Mathew was a good Archbishop, dealing tolerantly and sensibly with local Puritans and travelling regularly round his diocese to preach the gospel, despite the impression he gave that a sudden wind might blow him into eternity (**49**).

Richard Bancroft, James's first Archbishop of Canterbury, was an energetic reformer. The success of his drive against abuses is debatable, but he probably raised the general level of learning and conduct among the clergy (**28**). When he died in 1610, his successor was George Abbot, Bishop of London. Lancelot Andrewes was favourite for the vacancy, but his Arminian views were too 'high' for the Calvinist monarch who had no sympathy with his belief that the authority of bishops came from God. Abbot, who believed that episcopal authority derived solely from the Crown, was therefore a stronger candidate, and got the job. The new archbishop was a good and pious man, but because he neglected to carry out any drastic reforms, he has been compared unfavourably with Bancroft and given a bad press. He was, for a seventeenth-century prelate, properly involved in politics. At court he was one of the leaders of the anti-Spanish faction, and in parliament he succeeded in establishing better relations with the House of Commons than any archbishop since the death of Cranmer. These secular activities have been exaggerated as a result of an unfortunate accident in 1621 when, indulging in the unedifying sport of hunting, Abbot shot a keeper instead of a stag, and had to be temporarily suspended. When conscience demanded, he opposed the king. Abbot's refusal to annul the marriage of Lady Frances Howard to the Earl of Essex infuriated James, who had to pack the Commission with more compliant bishops (see p. 50). In 1618 Abbot again opposed the king, this time over James's *Book of Sports*, a declaration encouraging games on Sundays after church. On this, and on other matters such as the king's foreign policy and his toleration of Catholics, Abbot was in full agreement with the Puritans. As archbishop he conscientiously fulfilled his duties, carrying out a number of visitations in his diocese to make sure that the canons were being observed (72). He gently insisted on conformity while refraining from persecution. So although Abbot failed to achieve any dramatic reforms, he did succeed in bringing peace to the Church — no small achievement in the seventeenth century.

Most of the bishops were as concerned about the state of the Church as were the Puritans. The canons of 1604 insisted on high minimum qualifications for candidates for the ministry and tried to restrict pluralism. Both Bancroft and Abbot encouraged ministers either to preach every Sunday or hire, once a month, a man who could. Those bishops who were resident in their dioceses conducted visitations to search out papists and the more outrageous nonconformists; they licensed preachers and encouraged those who could not preach to read homilies instead. Men were ordained, schoolmasters approved, books licensed and children catechised. Although most dioceses await detailed study, the visitation records of Bancroft and Abbot echo those of the Elizabethan period, and the very persistence of the abuses bears witness to the tremendous difficulties of effective reform. Many of the Church's ills reflected the irremediable circumstances of society as a whole. As the output of clergy from the universities increased, more and more graduates had either to be content with poor livings, or to hold pluralities (84). The king himself regarded pluralism and non-residence as regrettable necessities to attract able graduates to holy orders. With 3,849 out of 9,000 livings impropriated to laymen, the creation of a learned — and therefore properly salaried — ministry would have required a massive onslaught at the whole system of lay patronage which, practically speaking, was out of the question (41). In theory one-tenth of a person's produce or income should have gone to the Church, but in practice only a fraction of this found its way to the clergy. Lay patrons usually paid only a proportion of the tithes they collected to the minister. Many tithes had been commuted in the past for money payments which had remained fixed in spite of inflation. When Archbishop Bancroft tried to use the Church courts to get out of date commutations revised and to extract tithes from hitherto exempt produce, he became entangled in legal disputes with Sir Edward Coke and the common lawyers (28).

Dissatisfaction with the government, ceremonies and faults of the Church continued throughout the reign. In 1606 and 1607 Puritan M.P.s received the support of a majority of their colleagues in an unsuccessful attempt to assist the ministers deprived for refusing subscription. An attack was launched against the Court of High Commission and its use of the notorious *ex officio* oath, which obliged the accused to swear to answer truthfully whatever questions he might be asked (70). Both Whitgift and Bancroft had used this oath to ask ministers if they were guilty of nonconformist (and punishable) practices. At the same time, and again in 1610, bills were passed to promote a preaching ministry and to discourage pluralism and non-residence, only to fail in the Lords. Anticlericalism and jealousy of Convocation rather than Puritan zeal may have encouraged many M.P.s to vote for these Bills, but their support of measures 'to prevent and reform profane swearing and cursing', for making the sabbath holy, for preventing ministers frequenting brothels and for restraining 'inordinate haunting and tippling in inns, ale houses and other victualling houses', suggests a moral earnestness very characteristic of the Puritan temperament.

In the parishes of England the conforming majority of Puritan ministers gave most of their attention, not to disputes over ceremonies, but to the pursuit of piety and to improving the morals and manners of their congregations. They did this by preaching and example, eventually acquiring a considerable influence in pulpit, Press, school and university (44). The desire of the laity for sermons (about 100 a week were preached in London in 1600) was partially satisfied by the creation of lectureships in towns all over England, but especially in London (63). Lecturers were unbeneficed clergy appointed exclusively to preach, and were financed by men committed to improving the Church. Naturally, the Puritans played a leading role in this development. Yet it was preaching that people wanted, and not necessarily Puritan preaching. One of the surprising results of Dr Seaver's research has been the discovery that in London during the years 1600-28 only 45 to 55 per cent of the lecturers were Puritans (63, p. 203). Until Archbishop Laud's primacy, little action was taken against them, probably because even a Puritan lecturer could preach godly sermons without attacking the establishment. As Queen Elizabeth had realised, what mattered was not preaching but what was preached, a subject which has not yet been thoroughly investigated. When, in the 1620s, the Palatinate crisis caused an outburst of preaching critical of the king's foreign policy and his leniency towards Catholics, James reacted by issuing his *Directions to Preachers* (1622) severely restricting the topics on which the clergy could preach. His *Book of Sports*, with its encouragement of Sunday games, also offended the godly.

The king's tolerant treatment of English Catholics gave offence to most of the political nation. The Papists had hoped for more in the way of toleration from James than they were to get (**102**). The inevitable disillusionment produced the rather feeble Bye Plot of 1604 and the much more formidable Gunpowder Plot of 1605. Although this plot was followed by a spate of savage penal legislation, James and Cecil were not anxious to persecute, recognising that the conspiracies were the work of a desperate minority. The government played on a division between the secular and regular clergy, and to widen the breach tried to devise an oath of allegiance which Catholic laymen and secular priests could take. The recusancy fine of £20 a month, or confiscation of two-thirds of a person's property for non-payment, legally enforceable on Catholics who refused to attend Anglican services, was seldom fully exacted. This gentle treatment was partly the result of James's tolerance and partly a necessary accompaniment to the long-drawn-out marriage negotiations with Spain (see ch. 7). Although twenty-eight Catholics were executed for treason during the reign, the failure to enforce the penal laws brought bitter complaints that the number of Papists was increasing. There were Catholics in high places; the number of priests grew, and in 1623 a newly appointed bishop divided England into seven vicariates and nineteen archdeaconries. To these twenty-six vicars-general and archdeacons he added a dean and 10 canons, and constituted them into a Chapter, with control over the secular clergy. Between 1607 and 1619 the Benedictine community in England was revived, while the Jesuits, who had been active throughout the previous reign, increased in number to over 140 by 1625 (**71**). So it was with some justification that parliament regularly complained at the spread of popery. By the end of the reign, these developments, together with the slow but perceptible growth of Arminianism, which threatened the theological unanimity of English Protestants, had to some extent revived the subversive elements of Puritanism that James had done much to contain.

7 Foreign Policy and the 1621 Parliament

PEACE WITH SPAIN

From 1585 until 1604 the English had fought Spain for the independence of their country and, with the Dutch, for the survival of Protestantism in northern Europe. By 1601 the country was heartily sick of war. The Crown was deep in debt. Elizabeth owed the City of London some £80,000 and another £120,000 was outstanding on privy seal loans. Parliament was quibbling about the queen's request for four subsidies and growling at her grant or sale of monopolies. In Ireland the prosecution of the war was hovering on the brink of disaster. By the end of the reign the debts had increased, but the tide had turned in Ireland. Spain was exhausted and the time was ripe for peace. King James wisely put an end to war in 1604, despite pressure from the Dutch to carry on. Henry IV of France, who felt that his own security depended upon Spain's continuing preoccupation with England and the Netherlands, also sent envoys to persuade James to keep fighting. But James refused to live at war so that Henry could live in peace. Instead, the two kings agreed that troops would continue to be raised in England and paid for by France, one-third of the outlay being credited as payment on the French debt still outstanding.

The peace treaty with Spain was not discreditable and did no damage either to the Dutch or the French. James made no significant concessions. Trade with the United Provinces and with the archduke's territories was to continue and English merchants were allowed to penetrate Mediterranean markets. Flushing and Brill, the cautionary towns held as security for the Dutch debt, remained in English hands. The Dutch would continue to recruit in England. The English were left to enjoy the benefits of peace in the comfortable knowledge that Spain was still at war with the United Provinces. Although it is often assumed that the peace treaty was unpopular, the evidence suggests that is was generally accepted as a sensible measure. Yet if the war was over, the tradition lived on. The heavy taxation, the miseries of war were quickly forgotten. A tiny minority of privateers and military persons resented being unable to attack Spain and the Indies. Such people, together with men like Sir Walter Raleigh, who wanted to found English colonies in

Analysis

America, were anxious for war to begin again. But these were men without influence. More dangerous were the myths. By the 1620s many M.P.s believed that the English navy had once chased the Spanish half way round the world, plundering treasure ships to help pay for war. Baiting Spaniards was firmly established as a national sport [docs. 14, 15]. James underestimated and at times ignored his subjects' distrust of Spain and Catholicism. He rarely undertook to explain his policies to parliament, an understandable and reasonable attitude, but hardly wise, when what he was doing ran counter to national prejudice. He schemed throughout his life to avoid war, pinning most of his hopes on an *entente* with Spain. His policy of peace and friendship with Spain was not liked by Englishmen, who were convinced that Spain had both the intention and the capability to strive for 'universal monarchy'. A Spanish conquest of north-west Europe was, in fact, unlikely. But it was at least possible and its consequences would have been momentous. That men thought it likely at the time helps to explain why the king's foreign policy was so unpopular.

Between 1604 and 1609 English foreign policy was determined by the continuing war between Spain and the United Provinces. Neither James nor Cecil had much of a policy towards France, Spain or the Netherlands, except to wait on events. Difficulties thrown in the way of merchants trading with Spain put a strain on Anglo-Spanish relations, a state of affairs thoroughly exploited by the French. Yet instead of coming to an understanding about how to deal with Spain and the Dutch, James and Henry IV became immobilised by mutual suspicion and dislike (48). Henry was convinced that while he was bearing the financial burden of the Dutch war, James was profiting from it. The English countered requests for a renewal of financial aid to the Dutch with demands for a repayment of money lent to France by Elizabeth. James, who had neither money nor inclination to give the Dutch anything more than moral and diplomatic support, decided that it was unnecessary to dole out subsidies, since the French could hardly afford not to do so. He may well have been right; but in 1609 the Dutch themselves took a hand and, with the Truce of Antwerp, brought the war to a temporary halt.

After 1609 there were many who feared that Spain would use the twelve year cessation of hostilities to recover something of her former strength. For France this possibility was particularly worrying because of the continued presence of Spanish soldiers in the Low Countries. England had emerged with a choice of allies and was courted by both France and Spain. Her choice, however, was more apparent than real. Any long-term alliance with Spain would mean abandoning the United

Provinces, to whom James was committed by Treaty. Although James was aware of the growing economic and colonial rivalry of the Dutch, any attempt to abandon them to the mercy of Spain would be extremely difficult for political and ideological reasons. Yet there was little hope of preserving the peace of Europe without Spanish cooperation. Hence the ambiguities, difficulties and inconsistencies of James's foreign policy after 1609, rooted as it was in caution, poverty and an earnest desire to keep the peace.

James has sometimes been criticised for what is called his failure to appreciate the contemporary decline of Spain and future strength of France. The criticism is misplaced. James had no illusions about either the hostile attitude or inherent weakness of the Spanish government; his agents kept him fully informed about both. Nor was he unaware of the potential danger from France, though he can hardly be blamed for failing to anticipate the greatness she achieved under Louis XIV. Sir George Carew, reporting to James in 1609, made full allowance for the internal difficulties of France, yet still considered the French 'the most dangerous neighbours that we have. The Almains are disunited; Denmark not potent; Spain remote and busied about other matters; but France gathering force as it were to wrestle with somebody' (31, p. 48). James took care to feed the anti-Habsburg feelings of Henry IV, insuring the future by trying to establish a permanent friendship with Spain.

James's understandable reluctance to undertake expensive initiatives in foreign policy and his willingness to accept, within limits, the leadership of the more decisive Henry IV, almost led him into the war which, above all things, he wanted to avoid. Fearing isolation, James reluctantly followed the French king when, in 1610 he confronted the Habsburgs over the Cleves–Jülich succession problem (48). Only the murder of Henry saved James from becoming involved in a general conflagration. After the assassination James settled back with relief into his rôle of peacemaker. English and Scottish troops assisted by the French and Dutch, drove the Archduke Leopold from Jülich, and after further discussions and delays this immensely complicated matter was settled when both the Catholic and Protestant sides agreed to a partition of the Duchies (Treaty of Xanten, 1614). The crisis revealed that trouble between the Protestant Union and the Catholic League could not be confined to the Habsburg empire. The situation in Germany was closely linked with international rivalries between Catholic and Protestant and with domestic rivalry between Bourbon and Habsburg. If Europe divided into two ideologically opposed camps, James would find it difficult to avoid being at the head of one of them. During Louis

XIII's minority France made some show of a rapprochement with Spain. The king, Winwood explained to the English ambassador to France, felt that 'the preservation of the welfare of Christendom . . . cannot but run a great hazard if Spain shall become incorporated with France' (**31**, p. 47). To prevent this a mutually defensive alliance was concluded between England and France in August 1610 which, to a limited degree, bound France to the Protestant side. In March 1612 James made a similar alliance with the Princes of the Protestant Union, thereby appearing to many, if not to himself, as leader of the anti-Habsburg powers. It now became difficult for James to reconcile attempts to mediate between two opposing sides with his rôle as leader of one of them.

GONDOMAR

James looked to matrimony to keep the peace. His daughter Elizabeth he married to Frederick, Elector Palatine of the Rhine, on St Valentine's Day 1613, amidst festivities of immense tedium and cost. His eldest son he hoped would marry a princess of Spain. Related thus to both Catholic and Protestant royalty, he would be in a strong position to mediate and pacify to his heart's content. As an ally, Spain was the obvious choice, since French prevarications, lasting more than a decade, over the repayment of money loaned to France by Elizabeth, did not inspire much confidence that an acceptable dowry would be negotiated from that quarter. Moreover, a marriage treaty with France might involve James in embarrassing promises to ignore whatever fate befell the Huguenots. Only a Spanish marriage would provide a large dowry and promote the cause of peace. The idea of marrying the Prince of Wales to a Spanish Princess had been suggested as early as 1604; thereafter both sides periodically produced the scheme from their diplomatic bags, dusted it and laid it open for inspection. The idea received new life with the arrival in England in 1613 of a new Spanish ambassador, Don Diego Sarmiento de Acuña. In 1617 Sarmiento became Count Gondomar; it is by this name that he is generally known and hereafter called.

Gondomar was a first class diplomat; shrewd, urbane, charming and polite. He had not been long in England before rumour had transformed him into 'the Spanish Machiavelli', manipulating James in the interests of Spain [doc. 14]. It is difficult to assess the accuracy of these rumours. Gondomar's opinions certainly carried weight and his susceptibilities were indulged. He was helped by the Spanish faction when their interests happened to coincide with his (**52**). Although many of the Howards and their friends were Catholics, they were not particularly zealous and had no wish to be 'liberated' by the Spanish. They were pro-Spanish mainly in the sense that they favoured an alliance with Spain rather than with France. Gondomar inherited pension obligations which were of little use but which could not be jettisoned for fear of making enemies. Cecil had been paid £1,500 a year by the Spanish, who considered him a bad investment. When he died, Somerset insisted on inheriting his pension and the Spanish were obliged to agree. In 1618 Buckingham in his turn received the 6,000 ducats a year. Such highly placed individuals gave poor value for money, doing no more than act as counterweights to those courtiers who were pro-French and 'Protestant'. Sir William Monson, commander of the channel fleet, was a better bargain, providing Gondomar with details of Dutch and English shipping. The pensioners had little or no effect on James's foreign policy, but they did occasionally provide Gondomar with useful information. The government could, however, guard against anything vital being leaked because, thanks to the vigilance of the English ambassador to Madrid, James had a copy of the pension list (101).

Gondomar's influence was due less to his cunning and James's gullibility, more to their long association and mutual respect. The king admired Gondomar and relished his company and conversation. They became good friends, called themselves 'the two Diegos' and were seen drinking from the same bottle. Although a full reassessment of Gondomar's influence must await the publication of Professor Carter's forthcoming biography, it would appear that James could never be relied upon to do what the Spaniard wanted (80). When, having failed to procure English support for a projected war against Spain in the Alps, some French envoys complained that they found James 'completely Spaniard', Gondomar was ruefully amused. When they referred publicly to James as 'Don Jacques', the ambassador reported to his king that he wished that this were so. Occasionally James was indiscreet, as when he revealed to Gondomar the terms of Sir Walter Raleigh's charter to fit out a gold-seeking expedition to the Orinoco. Gondomar had objected to the proposal, claiming that the Spanish had already established a settlement in the area. James, who was under pressure from the anti-Spanish faction to let the expedition sail, but who nevertheless wished to preserve good relations with Spain, extracted solemn promises from Raleigh that he would not attack the Spanish. One can only guess what James was doing. He certainly wanted gold, and may well have accepted Raleigh's assertion that his voyage of 1595 had established a claim to the Orinoco. He had no evidence that the Spanish had actually settled at San Thomé. If Raleigh could win territory, find gold mines and avoid a collision with the Spanish, James was willing to risk a quarrel with Madrid. When San Thomé was attacked and no gold found, the Spanish agreed that James could not be held responsible because they knew the terms under which Raleigh had sailed. Raleigh lost his head but Anglo-Spanish friendship was preserved.

Expecting a renewal of war with the United Provinces in 1621, the Spanish government had sent Gondomar to lead James – if not up the garden path – at least into a neutral position. A Spanish marriage would counter the Palatinate marriage, prevent an Anglo-French alliance and improve the position of English Catholics. There was nothing humdrum about Spanish expectations. Gondomar was possessed by the chimera of England's conversion to the Catholic faith. He reasoned that if England's future king became a Catholic then the English would become Catholic, too. He backed his argument with impressive but unrealistic statistics, estimating that in the kingdom there were 300,000 recusants together with 600,000 Catholics attending Protestant worship. If James could be persuaded to relax the penal laws, the country would gradually return to the true faith and elect a Catholic House of Commons. The best way, therefore, to secure the friendliness of England and her conversion, was to marry Prince Charles to the Infanta. In an age of *cuius regio eius religio* this idea was not as foolish as it sounds. But it was not rooted in reality; English Protestantism was much more firmly established than Gondomar realised. James, too, was eager to arrange a Spanish marriage. In Madrid the official attitude changed regularly with changes in circumstances and personnel. Nevertheless, the Spanish government continued to discuss terms, calculating that negotiations would help to keep James out of the quarrels that were brewing on the Continent. In May 1615, the English ambassador to Madrid, Sir John Digby, sent for his King's inspection the marriage articles which the Spanish had prepared. James was shocked by the conditions. The children of the marriage were to be baptised by a Catholic priest and educated by their mother. If, when they came of age, they wanted to be Catholics, they must not lose their right of succession. The Infanta's servants were to be Catholics and her chapel must be open to the public. The penal laws must be repealed and English Catholics allowed full freedom of worship. Each one of these proposals was political dynamite, and all were rejected by King James. Twice thereafter, in 1616 and 1617, the flagging negotiations were revived. Each time they floundered on the question of freedom of worship for English Catholics, a necessary condition if the Pope was to find the marriage acceptable. James was prepared to relax the penal laws but could not promise to repeal them since Parliament would never agree. In July 1618, Gondomar returned home on sick leave. The dream of a Spanish marriage faded with his departure, to be revived only when a crisis in Europe gave the negotiations a significance they did not have before.

THE PALATINATE CRISIS

The European war that men expected did not begin in the Netherlands, but began instead in Prague, where in 1618 the largely Protestant nobility of Bohemia rebelled against their newly elected king, the archduke Ferdinand of Styria, a Catholic and a Habsburg. While a Catholic army from Flanders went to Ferdinand's assistance, a Protestant army sent by Frederick of the Palatinate helped the Bohemian rebels. When, in August 1619, Ferdinand was elected Holy Roman Emperor, the Bohemians offered the crown to Frederick who, after some hesitation, accepted. The Emperor, who lacked the resources even to defend Vienna, received help from Maximilian of Bavaria by offering him the Upper Palatinate and Frederick's electoral title when the Bohemians were subdued. The Lower Palatinate, west of the Rhine, he offered to Spain, so that while he and the Duke of Bavaria attacked Frederick in Bohemia, the formidable Spanish general Spinola would launch a diversionary attack on the Palatinate. At this point, in March 1620, Gondomar returned to London, presumably to keep James quiet.

The possibility of a Spanish attack on the Palatinate was being openly discussed in 1620 and the threat of English intervention might well have prevented such a move. Yet with the Truce of Antwerp about to expire, the Palatinate was of great strategic value to the Spaniards and the temptation to invade must have been hard to resist. James allowed himself to be reassured by Gondomar's promise that the Palatinate would remain inviolate and is reported to have said: 'The Palatine is a Godless man and a usurper. I will give him no help. It is much more reasonable that he, young as he is, should listen to an old man like me, and do what is right by surrendering Bohemia, than that I should be involved in a bad cause. The Princes of the Union want my help, but I give you my word that they shall not have it' (**75**, p. 414). Although the king was referring to help for Bohemia and not for the Palatinate, such indiscretion is staggering, if, that is, it was an indiscretion. Spanish diplomats were less inclined to believe James than historians have been since. The archduke's envoy, for instance, took 'as an infallible maxim of state that this king governs himself in these affairs with much artifice' so that what he said about Frederick could not be believed until it was seen what he actually did (**31**, p. 187).

Analysis

The conversation with Gondomar, reconstructed from gossip picked up by the French ambassador, is difficult to reconcile with the measures James took to protect the Palatinate. In March Archbishop Abbot was allowed to collect for Frederick a voluntary contribution from the clergy. On 9 June Sir Horace Vere, with a regiment of 2,000 volunteers, was sent to occupy the fortresses of the Lower Palatinate. In July, when Spinola moved towards the Rhine, James wrote to the government in Brussels demanding to know what he was up to, only to be told that they did not know. When, during the third week of August, 20,000 Spanish troops entered the Lower Palatinate, resistance came only from an Anglo-Dutch force under Vere, firmly established in the key fortresses of Frankenthal and Mannheim. By November 1620 Frederick was a vagabond king, having lost Bohemia and half the Palatinate to the armies of the Catholic League.

The invasion of the Palatinate turned the conflict in Germany into a general European war. The Protestant powers could view with indifference backyard fights in Bohemia, but they could not ignore a Spanish occupation of the Palatinate. Fed by religious fears and political animosities, the war in Germany blazed up into a great conflagration which took thirty years to die out. James was determined not to burn his fingers. There were those who believed that his powers were failing. 'It seems to me', wrote the French ambassador,

> that the intelligence of this King has diminished. Not that he cannot act firmly and well at times when the peace of the Kingdom is involved. But such efforts are not so continual as they once were. His mind uses its powers only for a short time, but in the long run he is cowardly. His timidity increases day by day as old age carries him into apprehensions and vices diminish his intelligence (75, p. 412).

The king had only just recovered from a serious illness, having been 'at once troubled with the stone, the gout and a scouring vomit'. Yet if during convalescence he was often weary and irritable, James was not so irresolute as some writers have suggested. He was under considerable pressure, from the dominant anti-Spanish faction on the Council, from Buckingham, and from Elizabeth and her husband to sever all links with Spain. The London mob staged hysterical anti-Spanish demonstrations, while Archbishop Abbot ecstatically declared that the prophecies of the Book of Revelation were about to be fulfilled in the destruction of Catholicism. Preachers and pamphleteers raged against the Habsburgs with such 'extraordinary violence' that James issued a proclamation forbidding his subjects to write or preach on matters of state (112). While Londoners cheered, quieter voices no less persistent, urged caution. James lacked the means to meddle on the Continent. He had no army and the fleet was rotten, though in process of repair. The Treasury was empty. A war would be immeasurably, even ruinously, costly. Frederick he regarded as a foolish usurper, whose cause was neither just nor in England's interest to support. James's policy, therefore, matched England's resources and her needs. A declaration of war was neither wise nor feasible and James was right to reject it.

The war in Germany and the renewal, in 1621, of hostilities between Spain and the United Provinces caused a revival in England of the old panic fear of Catholicism. James's policy was consequently unpopular, its subtleties ignored. For a zealous minority, Protestantism was an act of war against Catholicism. They demanded open intervention against the Catholic armies, a Protestant crusade. James rode out the storm, insisting that England could not fight effectively except at immense cost. The Palatinate, he maintained, could be saved by negotiation. Furious at Gondomar's deception over Spinola's invasion, the king launched a diplomatic offensive that greatly alarmed Madrid. On 8 September a naval squadron under Sir Robert Mansell set sail for the Mediterranean, despite Gondomar's efforts to stop it. This was ostensibly part of a long-planned Anglo-Spanish attack on the Barbary pirates, but the threat implicit in Mansell's presence in the Mediterranean was not lost on Madrid. At the same time Albertus Morton, formerly James's agent in Heidelburg and now secretary to the Council, was sent to Germany to 'force and persuade' the princes of the Union to assist in the recovery of the Palatinate. If mediation failed, James promised to send in the summer of 1621 men and money to Frederick's aid. To make this possible, writs had gone out summoning a meeting of parliament for January 1621. Envoys from the United Provinces, who suggested an Anglo-Dutch invasion of Flanders to relieve pressure on the Palatinate, were favourably received at court and a Council of War established to plan and cost the campaign. To the Habsburgs, this was particularly alarming because in December 1620 James told the archduke that on the expiration of the truce he would be obliged to support the United Provinces. Volunteers were already being recruited at such speed that there was not a ship departing for Holland that did not carry sixty or seventy men. In the light of this activity it is hardly fair to indict James with 'sad irresolution' and 'a policy of drift' (**75**, p. 412). His strategy in 1620 was sound, obliging Spinola to abandon the conquest of the Palatinate before it was complete and return in haste to Brussels. James sincerely, and very sensibly in view of his financial predicament, wanted a negotiated settlement. Simultaneously he prepared for war. If this failed to secure Frederick's restoration, the marriage negotiations could be abandoned and the Palatinate regained by force.

In formulating tactics during the negotiations James depended on information he received from his agents in Madrid, who in 1621-22 were convinced that the Spanish intended to go through with the alliance, although in fact they had decided to do the opposite. When they sent to Rome a diplomat called Diego de la Fuente with instructions to persuade the Pope to refuse a dispensation, James was informed: 'The friar that came lately out of England (who was this king's agent there) is now going to Rome and they speak here of that business (the marriage) as if it were already effected' (31, p. 270). Later, when the Spanish agreed to restore Frederick, they could not do so because they were unable to make decisions that were binding on the emperor, who needed the Upper Palatinate to reward Maximilian of Bavaria. And so the marriage negotiations were likely, eventually, to fail. This made it all the more important for James to reach an understanding with the third parliament of his reign, which opened on 3 January 1621.

THE PARLIAMENT OF 1621

Parliament met during a trade depression of alarming proportions, which began in 1620 and lasted nearly four years (91). It hit rock bottom in 1621. Not everyone suffered from this slump, although most people were feeling the effects of a harvest failure of the previous year. Although a significant section of the population was engaged in the manufacture of textiles, the English economy was still characterised by regional variations. While local industries and subsistence farming were not crippled by the paralysis of London and the export trade, many rural areas suffered from the effects of the economic crisis; many towns and ports were badly hit, and there was a shortage of money, which forced down the price of land. Members of the House of Commons were probably more concerned with alleviating the depression than with helping Frederick. Nevertheless, this proved to be a busy and, until the end, cooperative parliament. Anxious to avoid a repetition of the 1614 fiasco, James had accepted the need for discreet preparations. Special commissioners prepared some Bills and urged a liberal policy. In his opening speech, James made clear his intention to negotiate rather than fight for Frederick, but asked for money so that he could argue with an army at his back. He anticipated criticism by promising to curb his generosity and by reminding parliament that the Treasury Commissioners had recently attacked administrative inefficiency. Finally, he invited the Commons to present their grievances and to scrutinise the activities of monopolists.

Having taken the initiative in this way, and backed by about 135 office holders in the Commons, the government might have expected a relatively smooth passage. The courtiers, however, despite their numerical strength, were not very effective in debate, while the nine privy councillors were divided among themselves. The Speaker, Sergeant Richardson, had never before sat in parliament and had but a poor grasp of procedure. Secretary Calvert was regarded as a 'hispaniolised Papist' and made little effort to spell out in detail the policies of the king. The three most able councillors were united only in their dislike of each other. Sir Edward Coke and the Lord Chancellor were old enemies, while Cranfield joined the pack that howled for Bacon's impeachment. Coke was the most effective parliamentarian of them all, but had quarrelled with James when he lost the Chief Justiceship in 1616. After failing to obtain the Treasury in November 1620 he openly opposed the government in the Commons, where his tactical skill and immense knowledge were of inestimable value in the campaign against maladministration. Thus the strength of the critics of the government lay chiefly in the weakness of the government. Phelips, Strode, Sandys and Coke clearly appreciated this weakness but made no attempt to organise themselves into anything like an effective opposition. Most of the county members, while favouring reform at home and help for Protestantism abroad, were chiefly concerned with local affairs.

The journals and diaries of this unusually well-documented parliament show how much time was spent on the reform of abuses which had little to do with matters of State. Although it is impossible in the space available to do justice to their debates, it is worth emphasising that as well as discussing monopolies, the depression, administrative corruption and foreign affairs, the House of Commons and its committees dealt with an impressively wide range of business. They discussed freedom of speech, the enforcement of the penal laws, drunkenness, profane-swearing, Sunday dancing, the manufacture of substandard salt, the abolition of trial by battle, and the repair of roads. They pressed for legal reform and tried to help the textile industry by forbidding the lower classes to wear silk and similar expensive materials. By the time they were adjourned on 4 June the Commons had given fifty-two Bills a second reading and had nearly fifty more in the pipeline (5, vii, 300-7). Unfortunately, the sudden dissolution that followed a row over privilege during the second session prevented any of these Bills receiving the royal assent.

The preoccupation of members of parliament with local affairs did not leave them indifferent to issues of national importance. To preserve the support of the county community which elected him, a member had to show a proper distaste for maladministration and high taxation. Yet despite some difficult moments, Sir Edwin Sandys in May 1621 could speak, with some justice, of the 'Unity talked of in all this country and in Christendom between the Houses and us and the King, and God forbid that there should be any breach between us' (5, iii, 192). James had been gratified when, on 15 February, the Commons had settled down to discuss his needs. The government was less than frank about what was required, possibly because the estimated cost of a war of intervention was so staggering. The Council of War had requested an army of 30,000 men at an immediate cost of £250,000. Later an annual sum of £900,000 would be needed. Calvert simply asked for £500,000 for an army of 30,000 men, arguing that although James desired peace he was willing to prepare for war. Had James made clear the true cost of intervention he might have spiked the guns of those who wanted him to lead a Protestant crusade. After some discussion, the Commons decided to grant two subsidies, 'neither for Defence of the Palatinate nor yet for relieving the King's wants, but only as a free gift and present of the Love and Duty of his subjects'. The king was delighted and assumed, from the tone of the debate and the wording of the subsidy Bill, that more subsidies would be forthcoming after grievances had been aired.

Monopolies were the most important grievance in 1621 and the first object of attack. The king, through the exercise of his prerogative, could grant courtiers the exclusive right to sell or manufacture selected articles. Whereas in the second half of the sixteenth century nearly 100 monopolies had been granted, James granted 108 in just over twenty years. Although some were designed to protect new industries, like the saltpetre monopoly of the Evelyn family which helped shelter the armament industry, some gave power to issue licences or to bend the law. Monopolists were widely regarded as men licensed by the king to enrich themselves at the expense of the consumer. In 1617 the Earl of Salisbury received £7,000 a year from the silk monopoly, the Earl of Northampton £4,500 from starch. The king, who granted monopolies, enforced them in the prerogative courts and bore the brunt of public hostility, received the smallest reward: of every 1*s* paid by the consumer to the monopolist, only 1½*d* went to the Exchequer: the remainder went into the pockets of patentees and courtiers. In 1621, when it was alleged that there were about 700 monopolies, the Commons objected to them on three counts. They put up prices, profited courtiers and seemed to be a form of taxation unauthorised by parliament.

In pursuing monopolists the Commons initiated some important procedural developments that considerably enhanced their power (89). A subcommittee examined complaints, collected evidence and issued executive orders. The most famous of the enquiries concerned the licensing of inns, a monopoly held by Sir Giles Mompesson, a kinsman of Buckingham. When a search for precedents revealed nothing that would justify the Commons punishing a man for offences committed out of parliament, they appealed to the Lords to condemn him. Although the peers refused to pass a Monopolies Bill condemning specific patents, they agreed to deal with Mompesson, thereby reviving the medieval practice of impeachment, last used to try Lord Stanley in 1459. This procedure, whereby the Commons presented their accusation, evidence and list of witnesses, and left the Lords to conduct the trial and pass sentence, was then used against a minister of the Crown. While condemning monopolists some members of the Commons wanted to attack the making of the grant as well. They were warned off this dangerous issue of prerogative and contented themselves with enquiring into the activities of Lord Chancellor Bacon, who was accused of accepting bribes from people whose cases were pending. There is nothing to suggest that these 'gifts' affected his legal judgment; indeed, he had often decided against those who gave him money, which possibly accounts for the vindictiveness of some of his accusers. Bacon was impeached by the Commons before the Lords, who fined him £40,000 and degraded him from office. By attacking the Lord Chancellor parliament had voiced its disapproval of corruption at court. The private war between Coke and Bacon inevitably played a part, perhaps even a major part, in the public ruin of the Chancellor. James showed himself to be aware of this when he asked parliament not to 'hunt after, nor snatch at Abuses, but do all for love of Justice, not for private purposes of Spleen'.

Although it is unlikely that impeachment was revived deliberately to embarrass the king, it was, from the Crown's point of view, an ominous development. Since 'corruption' was a charge easily levelled against any minister, parliament now had a weapon which was available so long as the king chose not to dissolve them. The precedent was sufficiently sinister to alarm James, who, when he agreed to punish Bacon, warned parliament not to 'abridge the Authority of Courts, nor my Prerogative'.

The 1621 parliament spent much of its time discussing the decay of trade (91). Whereas cloth exports from London rose from 112,785 pieces in 1600 to 127,215 pieces in 1614, by 1622 they had dropped to 85,741 pieces. The debates in 1621 give a clear impression of how serious the depression was even though they fail to analyse correctly the reason for the slump. The kingdom's prosperity depended to a dangerous degree on the export of cloth to northern Europe, an area particularly vulnerable to fluctuations in demand caused by economic or political disturbances. The most important single cause of this complex crisis was one such disturbance, namely attempts by foreign princes to make a quick profit by tampering with the coinage. In Poland and Germany the outbreak of the Thirty Years War was accompanied by currency debasements which caused great confusion in all currency and exchange dealings. English exporters discovered that their cloth brought them less silver than usual. The only way to avoid a loss was to increase prices, a step which struck a further blow at sales. Nor was the English textile industry well equipped to meet foreign competition by reducing costs; had it been able to do so the impact of foreign currency manipulations would have been correspondingly less (**67**).

Although it was the task of the Council to alleviate the depression, the House of Commons acted as a sounding board for grievances and possible remedies. It was not until members gathered at Westminster and pooled their tales of falling prices, unsold wool and the collapse of foreign markets, that the scale of the crisis became clear. A Commons committee invited representatives of the trading companies and of the clothiers of Kent, Worcestershire, Suffolk, Essex, Somerset and Gloucester to present evidence and discuss remedies for the depression. The investigation showed how dangerously dependent English exports were on foreign markets. Heavy export duties and the fact that most cloth exports were finished and dyed in Holland received critical attention. It was easier to talk about trade than to expand it. Part of the answer lay in the development of new trades and industries, in a search for new markets, in the creation of colonies and the development of a mercantile economy. Such answers were inevitably long-term and beyond the understanding of parliament. The ordinary back-bencher, as Chamberlain reported to his friend Dudley Carleton, felt that 'the realm was never so bare and poor since he was born'. In these circumstances it is not surprising that the gentry were reluctant to grant a generous supply.

Immediately before the first session ended, Sir John Perrot gravely directed the attention of the Commons to the dangers which threatened Protestantism at home and abroad. He suggested that if the Palatinate could not be recovered by negotiation, they should undertake to risk their lives and estates for Frederick's well-being. Perrot's motion received the enthusiastic assent of the House and was written out in the more formal language of a Declaration [doc. 11]. After the adjournment both king and Commons had cause to congratulate themselves. Having attacked corruption and granted two subsidies for the king's immediate needs, the Commons had twice indicated their willingness to make additional grants for the Palatinate. While the Commons spent sixteen weeks discussing grievances James had restrained what was probably a strong temptation to complain, knowing that he could look forward to receiving further subsidies at the second session.

During the adjournment efforts were made to improve trade along lines suggested by parliament. New restrictions were placed on the export of iron ordnance and of wool. Several committees were set up to advise the Council on the decay of trade and the scarcity of coin. Legal reforms received attention. Finally, on 16 June the king issued a proclamation which cancelled eighteen monopolies and listed seventeen against which anyone could appeal. The effect of these attempts to meet the wishes of parliament was spoilt when the Earl of Southampton and Sir Edwin Sandys were arrested for meeting secretly to discuss parliamentary business. Lord Oxford was detained for criticising the king's plan for a Spanish marriage. These men were soon released, but at a time when the government wanted a generous supply, the arrests made the Commons very sensitive about their privileges.

Meanwhile the situation abroad did not improve. In May 1621 James sent John Digby to Vienna to effect a reconciliation between Ferdinand and Frederick, but the truce he arranged was soon broken by both sides. While the Catholic League tightened their grip on the Palatinate, Mansfeld, Frederick's mercenary general, was driven back towards the Rhine. In October James decided to take firmer measures. Military preparations were begun, some money was sent to Frederick and parliament was recalled in November instead of the following February as previously intended. Assuming that the Commons would react swiftly to the crisis, honour their promises and provide him with money, James left London for Newmarket, where he remained throughout the session. But instead of agreeing to a request for money to support Frederick's army through the winter, together with an additional £900,000 in the spring to maintain an army for one year, the Commons discussed the arrests made during the adjournment. Only with difficulty were they persuaded to allow this subject to drop. When on 26 November they discussed supply their debate soon broadened out into an unprecedented examination of foreign policy, which revealed that although the Commons believed that the Palatinate ought to be saved they were not prepared to give the king the wherewithal to save it. Their reasons were not voiced in one unanimous bellow; for although the majority were united on issues like monopolies, they did not speak with one voice on the question of aid to the Palatinate.

The men usually regarded as leaders of opinion in the Commons differed in their response to the king's request for supply. Alford and Pym recognised that the House had a duty to help James fulfil his obligations to Frederick, but were alarmed at the crippling cost of war. Both emphasised the need to enforce the recusancy laws, a step that might well drive a wedge between England and Spain. Sir Edward Coke concentrated on the Spanish menace. He and Wentworth wanted to proceed with the business in hand before granting supply, and opposed the king's expressed wish that parliament should do no more than grant money for Frederick, leaving other matters until they met again in February. 'Adjournment upon adjournment, subsidy upon subsidy, and nothing done will make us ridiculous' grumbled Wentworth (5, v, 214). Phelips too, although he urged war against Spain, wanted parliament to remedy abuses before considering supply. Crew argued that the London merchants could lend money to Frederick; before parliament supported a war 'he desired the king would let us know the Enemy we must fight against'. Although he knew, like everyone else, that the enemy was the Catholic League, Crew wanted a breach with Spain. 'If we might have some assurance from his Majesty that we might see the Prince matched to one of the same religion, how glad it would make us and willing to give' (5, vi, 199). A handful of mavericks urged the Commons to consider a naval war of diversion which would sap the strength of Spain and pay the expenses of war. These men were deluded. They drew false conclusions from the activities of Elizabethan privateers and forgot that such activity had been accompanied by financial backing to the tune of two, three and finally four subsidies. But to a House more inclined to talk than pay, this scheme was attractive.

A majority of the Commons agreed that some money must be granted, though they did not, in their enthusiasm, lose control of their purses. Their concern for Protestantism was not matched by a desire to pay the heavy price of intervention on the Continent. In a fit of midsummer madness they had promised to risk their lives and fortunes to recover the Palatinate. But words are cheap, military action costly. By November they heartily agreed with Sir George More, who demanded action but was reluctant to pay; of the estimated £900,000 he seems never to have heard. 'Let's still follow the King with our protestation of life and fortune', he said, wondering whether one subsidy would be too much. Perhaps a fifteenth would do. 'We must remember that we are sent by others. What we give they must pay' (5, iii, 464). It seems likely that Sir George mirrored the views of a majority of backbenchers. A reluctance to face their constituents having done nothing but recommend heavy taxation during a period of depression, this, rather than a distrust of the king, may account for the contrast between the strong words and limp actions of the 1621 parliament. Although the Commons had promised to assist Frederick 'with their lives and fortunes', they now decided to grant one subsidy for the support of the troops already in the Palatinate 'till the King can have an account of his treaties; then at our next meeting to give as the affairs shall require; and this will be for two or three months' (Phelips). The grant, small as it was, presumably satisfied those who believed that parliament was obliged to help the Palatinate, as well as those who thought that the settlement of grievances should come before supply (5, iii, 463).

The threads of this important debate were drawn together in a petition discussed by the Commons on 3 December (12). This remarkable and startling document expresses a deep concern for the future of Protestantism in Europe, hostility to Spain and a desire for a cheap war. The king's preference for negotiation was criticised. He was asked to save the Palatinate by force of arms, marry Prince Charles to a Protestant and enforce the recusancy laws. The idea of a maritime war of diversion was given a prominent place. Although this idea had not received much support during the debate, it was presumably taken up because the Commons could not reasonably advocate war without providing the money. Some of the more cautious members felt uneasy about the petition while the courtiers vigorously opposed it. Sir Robert Bevill had already told the subcommittee which had prepared the petition that he feared they were too bold about the Prince's marriage. The debate now centred on this point, which was clearly an infringement of the prerogative. Wentworth and Phelips suggested that they present it as advice, without asking for an answer; and before the petition was passed a few words were added to mitigate the offence: 'This is the sum and effect of our humble declaration which (no way intending to press upon your Majesty's most undoubted and regal prerogative) we do with the fullness of all duty and obedience humbly submit to your most princely consideration.' Before the petition could be presented, however, a letter was received from James forbidding the Commons to meddle in matters of State and reproving them for their abuse of Spain. He also told them 'that we think ourself very free and able to punish any man's misdemeanor in Parliament, as well during their sitting as after'.

Dismayed, and in some confusion, the House composed a second, explanatory petition which was delivered to James at Newmarket on 10 December. They excused themselves for discussing recusancy and the Spanish match on the grounds that both were connected with the defence of the Palatinate, and they introduced a new point of issue by claiming that the king's letter 'doth seem to abridge us of the ancient Liberty of Parliament for freedom of speech, jurisdiction and just censure . . . *the same being our ancient and undoubted right, and an inheritance received from our ancestors*'. The king's reply, carried back to Westminster and read on 14 December, was severe. Their attempt to direct foreign policy would invest them with 'all power upon earth, lacking nothing but the Pope's to have the keep also both of heaven and purgatory. . . . And therefore we have justly rejected that suit of yours: for what have you left unattempted in the highest points of sovereignty in that petition of yours except the striking of coin?' A 'hot persecution of our Recusants' he refused, because it would help turn a political struggle involving Germany, Spain and the Palatinate into an ideological struggle between Catholics and Protestants. The war in Germany, he reminded them, had little to do with religion but was the consequence of Frederick's usurpation of the Bohemian Crown. Their claim that parliament's privileges were 'an ancient and undoubted right and inheritance' he gently refuted, saying he would 'rather have wished that ye had said, that your Privileges were derived from the grace and permission of our Ancestors and Us. . . . Yet we are pleased to give you our Royal assurance, that as long as you contain yourselves within the limits of your Duty, we will be as careful to maintain and preserve your lawful liberties and privileges, as ever any of our Predecessors were, nay, as to preserve our own Royal Prerogative' (**79**, pp. 156-70).

The king was right and knew it: his firm reply with its gracious conclusion almost resolved the crisis. Debated favourably on the 14th, it received a much sharper response the following day. The Commons were urged by Phelips, Mallory and Seymour to put their privileges in writing – not provocatively in a Petition, but quietly in their own Journal, to put the record straight. On 18 December a Protestation was debated by no more than a third of the total membership of the Commons, approved and entered in the Journal of the House [**doc. 12**]. It claimed

that the liberties, franchises, privileges and jurisdictions of Parliament are the ancient and undoubted birthright and inheritance of the subjects of England; and that the arduous and urgent affairs concerning the King, State and defence of the realm and of the Church of England, and the maintenance and making of laws, and redress of mischiefs and grievances which daily happen within this realm, are proper subjects and matters of counsel and debate in Parliament.

The king ordered an adjournment as soon as he heard of the Protestation. On 30 December he announced his intention to dissolve parliament and, calling for the Journal, ripped out the page of protest with his own hand.

King and Commons had worked amicably together in 1621 until James questioned the unprecedented meddling of the Lower House in affairs of State. Knowing that the king's case was sound, the Commons might just have accepted a carefully phrased rebuke. But coupled with the rebuke was the threat: 'that we find ourself very free and able to punish any man's misdemeanours in Parliament'. The House could not ignore this claim. During the first session Alford had complained that 'there were eyes over him to observe'. Sir Francis Seymour claimed that he had been threatened with questioning 'after the parliament in another place' (5, vi, 220). This, and the arrest of Sandys, Southampton and Oxford during the summer recess, underlined the seriousness of the king's statement. The vehemence of the Commons' reaction suggests not only strength of feeling, but also relief that the focus of disagreement had shifted from their criticisms of foreign policy to the king's interference with the liberties of parliament. Having raised the question of privilege, the king had no alternative but to stand firm. He could not accept the Protestation. To the Commons, it was a 'conservative' document which did not claim new rights but defended privileges already possessed. To the king, it was a truly revolutionary statement in which the Commons infringed upon the powers of the Crown in terms which overrode all traditional restrictions. Unfettered freedom of debate and freedom from arrest were not 'the ancient and undoubted birthright and inheritance of the subjects of England'. Such claims, if accepted, would enlarge the function of parliament. So James 'rent out' the offending page from the Journal, not in rage, but solemnly, as an act of State, in the presence of his Council and the Judges. After the dissolution the government tried hard to raise money for the Palatinate by doubling the impost on wine and by launching a benevolence, which produced little more than the value of a subsidy. All hope of sending an army to the Palatinate had to be abandoned and James resorted, once again, to negotiating with Spain.

8 Foreign Policy and the 1624 Parliament

THE JOURNEY TO MADRID

Although by 1622 the Spanish match was an old, soiled project of eighteen years' growth, the failure of the 1621 parliament led James to revive the negotiations. The aim of English diplomacy was to arrange a marriage and to press for the restitution of the Prince Palatine. The Earl of Bristol, James's ambassador in Madrid, was instructed to negotiate two treaties:

> My instructions under your Majesty's hand were, to insist upon the restoring of the Prince Palatine, but not so as to annex it to the treaty of the match, as that thereby the match should be hazarded; for that your Majesty seemed confident, they here would never grow to a perfect conclusion of the match, without a settled resolution to give your Majesty satisfaction in the business of the Palatinate (Bristol to King James, 24 October 1623, **61**, p. 25).

In August 1622 James was invited to mull over the Pope's terms for a dispensation, which arranged the details of the Infanta's daily worship and her household, gave her control of her children's education until the girls were twelve and the boys fourteen, and demanded the repeal of the penal laws. Having replied that he could do no more than promise to suspend these laws, James went on to make equally impossible demands. The capture of Heidelburg led the king to ask for its restitution within seventy days. Should the emperor refuse, the Spanish must take the field against him. Although letters were sent to the emperor and to the Duke of Bavaria asking them to raise the siege of Frederick's fortress at Mannheim, the Spanish were unable to give James much satisfaction. Heidelburg was not restored. The siege of Mannheim continued and on 28 October the city fell. Tilly immediately marched on Frankenthal, the only fortress left to Frederick. In November the emperor announced that he intended to deprive Frederick of his electoral powers and confer them on Maximilian of Bavaria. At this point Philip despaired of marrying his sister to an

Englishman. Writing to Count Olivares, his chief minister, he said:

> My father declared his mind at his death bed concerning the match
> with England, which was never to make it; and your uncle's inten-
> tion, according to that, was ever to delay it; and you know likewise
> how averse my sister is to it. I think it now time to find a way out of
> it; wherefore I require you to find some other way to content the
> King of England, to whom I think myself bound for his many
> expressions of friendship (**36**, iv, 390).

Negotiations, however, did not cease. In spite of every reverse, James
was as anxious as ever to have the dowry and to procure Spanish
mediation in Germany. To Philip, the negotiations seemed the best way
of preventing English intervention in the war against the Netherlands.
With the advantage of hindsight one can see that in 1622 there was
little chance of a marriage and less chance of restoring Frederick. While
James exaggerated the extent of Spanish influence on the Emperor, and
although he had no knowledge of Philip's real views, on the evidence
available he could reasonably conclude that progress was being made.
The Spaniards had made concessions. They offered a dowry of
£600,000 and in December 1622 ceased to demand the repeal of the
penal laws, contenting themselves with a promise that James would not
persecute Catholics. The Earl of Bristol was assured that Philip would
do his best to put an end to fighting in the Palatinate and was shown a
letter which urged the Pope to approve the revised articles and to grant
quickly a dispensation. It is hardly surprising that James failed to see
through this carefully contrived deception but instead added new
towers to his castle in the air.

Then suddenly, in February 1623, Prince Charles decided to be his
own ambassador. Ludicrously disguised, calling themselves Tom and
Jack Smith, and travelling with only two companions, Charles and the
Marquis of Buckingham planned to ride through France to Madrid,
bring the flagging negotiations to a brisk conclusion and return
triumphant with the bride. The king's objections were brushed aside
and on 17 February the adventurers set out. Such a trip would have
been sensible only if the treaty had already been signed. In the circumstances it was foolish. English public opinion would be outraged, the
heir to the throne endangered and the Spaniards given an immense
diplomatic advantage since, with the prince in their hands, they could
make new demands on behalf of English Catholics. Although contemporaries blamed Gondomar and Buckingham for prompting the
idea, courtiers like Sir Henry Wotton and Bishop Goodman believed
that Charles himself was the instigator of the scheme. The ultimate

responsibility must rest with James, whose inability to refuse the request of his 'sweet boys' led to the ruin of his diplomacy. As the Spanish celebrated the arrival of their guests, a deep gloom fell on the English captial. James became ill with anxiety and busied himself with the therapy of despatching servants, chapel furnishings and Protestant chaplains to attend the prince of Spain. All he had to console him were his memories. 'I wear Steenie's picture in a blue ribbon under my wash-coat next to my heart', he wrote.

The arrival of Charles in Madrid caused the Spanish to reconsider their objections to a marriage. They did so because, as Francisco de Jesus in his account of the negotiations points out, Charles would never have risked coming to Spain had he not intended to dissolve all difficulties by becoming a Catholic (15). The English too suspected this. So while Londoners petitioned the Lord to deliver their prince from the clutches of the scarlet woman, the people of Madrid prayed earnestly for his conversion. Although James told his son to glory in his Protestantism, the prince did not immediately tell the Spanish that his conversion was impossible. Thus during the first few weeks of his stay in Madrid, Philip IV and Olivares were convinced that a marriage would take place just as soon as Charles became a Catholic. The Palatinate question would be settled along lines already explored by the diplomats. Frederick would surrender his claim to both Bohemia and the Electorate and send his nine-year-old son to Vienna, where he would eventually marry an archduchess, presumably having become a Catholic. After this marriage the Upper and Lower Palatinate would be restored to him, together with the Electorate when Maximilian died. This scheme was never really viable because neither Frederick, Ferdinand nor Maximilian would cooperate.

By the end of March the Spaniards had realised that Charles's religious convictions would not be shaken. While Olivares and his king had again decided that the marriage was off, they had no intention of infuriating Charles and his father by telling them so. The risk of war would be reduced if someone else could be blamed for the breakdown of negotiations. So the Duke of Pastrana went to Rome and asked the Pope to refuse a dispensation. Instead, His Holiness agreed to the marriage if stringent conditions were fulfilled. Fearing that promises made in Madrid would not be kept when Charles got home to London, he insisted that Philip should solemnly swear to ensure that the English carried out their obligations. The other conditions were based on the draft treaties of the past decade. The Infanta was to control the tutelage of future heirs to the English throne in a Catholic household until they were twelve. According to secret articles, James was to grant

Catholics a 'perpetual toleration' to worship in private and must promise to persuade parliament to repeal the penal laws. No attempt was to be made to convert the Infanta to Protestantism and no Bill against Catholics was to receive the royal assent. These conditions were so outrageous that they can only have been designed to exasperate the English into breaking off negotiations. While they waited for James's reply, a Junta of forty theologians solemnly laboured over how Philip's oath to the Pope might best be kept. The Infanta, they decided, must remain in Spain for at least a year after the marriage ceremony to give James time to effect the required conditions.

Prince Charles would inevitably reject these unacceptable conditions; or so it seemed to reasonable men. But Charles was no longer reasonable. He was in love, inflamed by the Infanta's inaccessibility. In London, having received both the marriage articles and the Junta's decision, the king wrote:

> But as for my advice and directions that ye crave, in case they will not alter their decree, it is, in a word, to come speedily away, and if ye can get leave, give over all treaty. And this I speak without respect of any security they can offer you, except ye never look to see your old dad again, whom I fear ye shall never see if you see him not before winter. Alas, I now repent me sore that ever I suffered you to go away. I care for match, nor nothing, so I may once have you in my arms again. God grant it, God grant it, amen, amen, amen.

After receiving this letter Charles made one last attempt to win concessions. Having failed, on 7 July he announced his capitulation, agreeing to everything the Spanish asked. He received nothing in return except the promise, twelve months hence, of a bride. In London, on 20 July, fearing for his son's safety, James signed the marriage treaty [**doc. 16**]. All the devils in hell, he said, and all the Puritans in England would not stop the marriage now. They did not need to, for by the time he had reached home, Charles was thinking more of his recent humiliation than of his future wife and was determined to salvage something from the wreck he had made of his father's diplomacy. There can be little doubt that Charles was primarily responsible for what had happened in Madrid. In April he had ignored Buckingham's advice to leave, thereafter conducting the negotiations himself, replacing the mandarin calm of Bristol's diplomacy with his own brand of irresponsible haggling. He became so unhinged by the prospect of matrimony that he failed to mention any other matter until after the treaty was signed. As Bristol later asserted, the Palatinate question was brushed aside because, as the duke put it, they came 'to woo and make love, and not to make war'.

The prince's behaviour bleached all meaning from his father's diplomacy. In letters to his son James had emphasised the importance of securing agreement on the dowry, the Palatinate and the date of the marriage. After signing the treaty Charles concentrated on persuading the Spanish to allow the Infanta to return with him to England. Philip adamantly refused. It was not until mid-August that Charles raised the question of the Palatinate. All that Olivares could offer was the scheme, already suggested at ambassadorial level, of eventually restoring Frederick's son after he had been educated in Vienna. In the meantime, Philip offered to try to persuade the emperor to return Frederick's lands. Charles was compelled to realise at the end of the negotiations what he should have seen at the beginning. Philip could not force a settlement on the emperor. According to Buckingham, Count Olivares had told them: 'We have a maxim of state that the King of Spain must never fight against the Emperor. We cannot employ our forces against the House of Austria' (**61**, p. 21). So long as the overland route from Spain to the Netherlands was secure, the Spanish were prepared to restore a chastened and dependent Frederick. Yet they could do nothing about the Upper Palatinate without the cooperation of Ferdinand, and he acted independently of Spain just as Frederick acted independently of England. Although it was naïve of the English not to grasp these facts at the start, it is incredible that Charles should have spent nearly six months in Spain before mentioning the Palatinate when his father and half of Europe were thinking of it daily. The Spanish account of the negotiations indicates that Olivares expected Charles to discuss the Palatinate at the start and was very surprised when the prince failed to do so (**15**). If Charles had seriously intended the restoration of Frederick to be a condition of the marriage, it should have been written into the marriage treaty from the beginning.

THE PARLIAMENT OF 1624

When Charles and Buckingham reached London in October 1623 they pretended to have been ill-used in Spain and persuaded James to bully the Spanish into restoring Frederick. The Earl of Bristol was forbidden to use the proxy for Charles's marriage to the Infanta and was instructed to procure from Philip 'a punctual answer what course he will take for the Restitution of the Palatinate and Electorate to our Son-in-Law; and, in case that either the Emperor or the Duke of Bavaria will oppose any Part of the expected Restitution, what course the King will take' (**61**, p. 20). James had at last joined together what had been two separate treaties; the restoration of the Palatinate was to be a condition of the marriage. While James continued to work for a negotiated settlement of the German question, Charles and Buckingham became convinced that only war against Spain would solve the problem. They pressed unremittingly for a parliament, confident that the Commons would help them snatch control of foreign policy from the hands of the king. Having given his consent (28 December), James sank into a gloomy — though temporary — paralysis, leaving his son and the favourite to pursue their policy of war against Spain. The foundations of a working partnership between Buckingham's faction and the popular leaders in parliament were laid, Bristol recalled to give an account of his embassy, and the governments of France, Venice and the Netherlands invited to join an alliance for the recovery of the Palatinate.

It is often assumed that James might just as well have been dead in 1624, so small was his influence on affairs. Dr Ruigh's study of the 1624 parliament has demonstrated that, on the contrary, the king still played an important and, at times, decisive part in the formulation of policy (**61**). Whereas Charles and Buckingham intended parliament to finance a war against Spain, the king intended to use parliament's bellicosity as a weapon of diplomacy to convince the Spanish that only Frederick's restoration would avert a declaration of war. If Frederick's restoration was not achieved with Spanish help then James would fight — not at sea against Spain, but in Germany against the emperor. When on 19 February James told both Houses: 'I assure you ye may freely advise me', and promised a full account of the negotiations in Madrid, he made it abundantly clear that they were to advise and not decide whether to break the treaties with Spain. On 24 February Buckingham held forth concerning his Spanish adventure, skating over why the Prince went to Madrid at all, and giving an impression that the restoration of the Palatinate had been closely linked to the marriage throughout the negotiations. He placed all blame for the fiasco on the perfidy of the Spanish, an argument loudly echoed by those M.P.s who rose and bobbed in his wake.

On 1 March Sir Benjamin Rudyerd, a client of the Earl of Pembroke, gave notice of the uneasy alliance between his master and the Duke of Buckingham by denouncing Spain. 'If we break off the treaty we must make good the breach; we must maintain it, and the likliest way is by a war, which is the manlier and more English way.' Rudyerd then suggested that the government should organise a Protestant confederacy, send an army to the Low Countries, garrison Ireland and repair the fleet. Attacks could be launched against Spanish colonies and shipping 'by way of diversion to save charges'. Sir Robert Phelips described the treaty as 'Spain's best army'. He expressed sorrow for the loss of the Palatinate and added:

> If we talk of revenge, yet whither should we look but towards him that hath wounded us. Spain is the great wheel that moves the whole frame of that business. They cannot, they will not restore it to us. It concerns Austria and Rome too much to part with it, and all these depend on Spain. For Spain and Rome are like the twins that laugh and weep and live and die together. There is no hope to gain it by treaty. Then we must war for it, or something better than it. Spain must be the enemy.

Although most other speakers recommended a dissolution of the treaties and war against Spain, this unanimity may have been more apparent than real. As Dudley Carleton observed (5 March), the fervour of the anti-Spanish M.P.s and the knowledge that both the prince and the duke desired a war probably influenced 'those that by the consideration of the whole charge of war like to rest upon their shoulders, were wavering and ready to advise the continuence of the treaty of restitution' (**61**, pp. 179-83).

Buckingham at this point gave public support to the idea of a diversionary war, presumably because, as lord admiral, he could expect a rich share of the plunder. Much depended on whether James could be persuaded to give a favourable answer to parliament's petition for a dissolution of the treaties. When the king refused to see Buckingham, spending time each day with the Spanish envoys, he received a furious and impertinent letter from the favourite [**doc. 17**]. A memorandum from the duke listing the concessions which James could make in his reply to parliament received scant attention [**doc. 18**]. Instead, the king reiterated his reluctance 'without Necessity, to embroil myself with War'. He complained of his insolvency, and hinted that the Spanish had given 'no small hope' for the restitution of the Palatinate (a reference to Philip's offer on 14 January to surrender the Lower Palatinate in August and to try to persuade the Emperor to hand over the rest). Shrewdly, James emphasised the expense of war, claiming that poverty made him reluctant to break off negotiations. This speech, together with an account from Cranfield of the heavy expenditure on foreign affairs since Michaelmas 1619, cooled the ardour of some M.P.s. Sandys, for instance, argued that a war must await a categorical refusal to restore the Palatinate; in the meantime parliament should concentrate on the redress of grievances. Everyone was aware that James would not abandon negotiations unless he was promised money with which to wage war. So on 11 March the House voted 'that in pursuit of our advice we will be ready (upon his Majesty's declaration to dissolve both treaties) to assist his Majesty with our persons and abilities in a parliamentary course'. Again, the king refused to be manoeuvred into a premature declaration of war. He would see the colour of their money first. For the 'great business' he would need five subsidies and ten fifteenths, together with one subsidy and two fifteenths annually until his 'crying debts' were paid. Only then would he be in a position to follow their advice. Buckingham and Charles did their best to explain away this unsatisfactory answer and badgered the king to change his mind. On 17 March they succeeded in obtaining from James a letter stating:

That he was resolved both in his conscience and honour to make instant war.
That he did desire to confer with them for the manner of that war.
That he did refuse to demand any subsidies for his debts and desired that his former demand of one subsidy and two fifteenths might be added to the great business of the war, and so to make six subsidies and twelve fifteenths.
That he would have one session at Easter, another at Michaelmas, and another in the spring (**61**, p. 215).

Triumphantly, the anti-Spanish elements pressed their advantage. Yet the unprecedented financial demands, estimated by Coke at £900,000, worried many M.P.s. The king's preference for a campaign on the Continent was well known, but it would cost less to attack Spain. 'Are we poor?' asked Eliot. 'Spain is rich. There are our Indies.' After a long debate, three subsidies and three fifteenths were voted, a less than adequate sum of about £300,000.

Military preparations could not commence until the subsidy Bill had passed both Houses. The Commons refused to be hurried, for 'if the Bill of subsidy went thus on winged feet, and other Bills of grace on leaden ones' there was no guarantee that grievances would be remedied. So recusancy was discussed, a petition presented and much constructive business undertaken. A standing commission on trade, set up in 1622, heard evidence from a Commons committee and took a number of sensible measures to improve trade. Legislation uncompleted at the time of the 1621 dissolution was now enacted, including Bills to restrict monopolies, reform legal procedures and to repeal many obsolete statutes. The rate of interest was reduced to 8 per cent. The spate of legislation and the work of the special committees on the cloth trade, monopolies and the economic situation, show what could be achieved when Crown and Commons cooperated. The reign ended with parliament committed to financing 'a real war'; but where, how and against whom was not made absolutely clear.

Although it is difficult to generalise about the wishes of all from the speeches of a few, usually militant M.P.s, there is little doubt that the leaders of the Commons intended supply for a war against Spain. Yet to have written this into the subsidy Bill would have caused the sort of row over privilege which they all wanted to avoid. When on 23 March James accepted their offer of money and promised to dissolve the treaties, he had warned them not to trespass on the prerogative by meddling in the prosecution of the war [doc. 19]. The Commons nevertheless pushed to the limit the concessions won from the Crown. The treaties were declared to be utterly dissolved and a Council of War was nominated. These councillors, and the commissioners responsible for collecting and expanding the subsidies, were made accountable to parliament. The money was described as 'first fruits' and was given for 'the support of the war that is likely to ensue, and more particularly for those points proposed by your Majesty; namely the defence of this realm, the securing of Ireland, the assistance of your neighbours, the states of the United Provinces and other of your Majesty's friends and allies, and the setting forth of your royal navy'. There is nothing here about a war at sea; but neither is there any mention of the Palatinate. There can be no doubt that everyone was fully aware of the king's intentions when they promised aid, for James had incisively and repeatedly stated that the subsidies were for military and diplomatic activity on the Continent that would directly assist the Palatinate. On 8 March he had addressed both Houses on the need to help his allies (13, iii, 250). On 14 March he outlined the nature and scope of his policy, emphasising that his aim was to restore the Palatinate, not to fight the Spanish at sea (13, iii, 265). When, on 29 May he gave thanks for the subsidies, he said 'that the money would be wholly employed to the use it was given . . . and insisted particularly and largely upon the recovery of the Palatinate (although that be not specified in the act)' (*Sir Francis Nethersole to Sir Dudley Carleton*, 2 June 1624, 61, p. 255).

The king's purpose then, was plain and the Commons knew it when they pledged their aid. On the other hand, a majority of speakers in the subsidy debate had indicated that 'the war likely to ensue' should be against Spain, though the conservatism of the majority had prevented this being mentioned in the Bill for fear of trespassing on the prerogative. When James asked the Commons to qualify assistance to the Low Countries with the phrase 'as a means to recover the Palatinate' he was refused. The ambiguity of the subsidy Bill caused difficulties in the next reign. The subsidies were described as 'first fruits of our hearty oblation' and were granted 'for the present', with a clear implication of more to come. 'We your loyal and loving subjects will never fail to assist your Majesty in a parliamentary way.' Yet when, in 1625, King Charles asked the Commons to fulfil this promise so solemnly made, they refused. They did so partly because they were being asked to finance a policy which in 1624 they had not approved, and partly because they were angered by a toleration of Catholics granted by the French marriage treaty.

THE IMPEACHMENT OF LORD TREASURER MIDDLESEX

As the government prepared for war, the Commons launched the impeachment of Lionel Cranfield (**59**, pp. 441-68). The Lord Treasurer's remorseless economies had made him many enemies, and when he remained obdurate in his opposition to war, Buckingham too turned against him. The attack on the Treasurer was skilfully orchestrated by the Buckingham faction. On the same day as Cranfield was denounced by Sir Miles Fleetwood in the Commons for having taken 'three or four great bribes', a committee report to the Lords blamed the deplorable state of Ordnance on Cranfield's fraudulence. When, early in May, Buckingham became seriously ill, Prince Charles led the prosecution in the Lords and, according to the Spanish ambassador, held meetings with members of parliament at night. Yet it was not easy to make the charges stick. The evidence of customs farmers who claimed to have paid bribes of £500 apiece was confusing and contradictory, so that the impeachment planned for 29 April had to be postponed until 7 May, while committees scrabbled in the mud for more evidence. The Treasurer's one hope was the king's continuing support. But the king, away at Theobalds, was slow to act. It would have been difficult enough to squash the charges at the outset, but by the time James intervened the only way to save Cranfield was by dissolving parliament. Nevertheless, while assuming the proper role of impartiality, the king courted many of the nobility to take Cranfield's part, but without much success. On 5 May he addressed the Lords and spoke warmly of his Treasurer, arguing that 'all Treasurers, if they do good service to their master, must be generally hated', although this was no reason to punish the defendant.

Contemporaries felt that James's speech did Cranfield little good; yet the king did make it clear that some of the charges involved actions which he himself had approved. Nevertheless, parliament was to discover the truth about the rest. Ominously the king observed that 'If of an Angel he became a Devil, I will never excuse him. I will never maintain any Man in a bad Cause.' Not only did James fear that his

Treasurer was unjustly accused, he was also disturbed by the implications of the alliance of court faction with parliamentary opposition that was intent on Cranfield's destruction. ' "By God, Steeny", he is reported to have said, "you are a fool, and will shortly repent this folly, and will find that in this fit of popularity you are making a rod with which you will be scourged yourself." And turning in some anger to the Prince, he told him that he would live to have his belly full of parliaments' (4, i, 37). Whether this is James's foresight or Clarendon's hindsight, impeachment had been twice used in three years against a minister close to the throne, an alarming development from the Crown's point of view. When Cranfield was reproved by the Lords for his behaviour as Master of the Wards and found guilty of extortion, bribery and mismanagement of the Ordnance department, Bishop Williams was sent by Buckingham and Charles to massage the king's tender conscience, just in case he made difficulties. 'Necessity', murmured the bishop, 'must excuse you from Inconstancy or Cruelty.' Sadly the king accepted the outcome of the trial. Middlesex was to lose all offices for ever, to be imprisoned in the tower during the king's pleasure and to be fined £50,000.

Cranfield's biographer has found him technically innocent of the particular charges brought against him though guilty of graft and extortion. The vices he attacked so successfully in others he had continued to practise himself. When in 1614 he ceased to be a merchant he had an income of £833 per annum from offices and pensions and £1,500 from rents; by 1618 his profits from office were £4,100 and in 1624 had climbed to £20,900 with £7,103 from rents (59). By shutting off the rewards of courtiers while at the same time keeping a portion of their surrendered revenues for himself, he made some implacable enemies. By allowing the import of Spanish tobacco in 1622 he had undermined the prosperity of the Virginia Company. A year later he played a leading part in exposing the shifty financial dealings of two of its directors, Sir Edwin Sandys and Sir Nicholas Ferrar. Cranfield fell, however, not because he made enemies but because he opposed the Duke of Buckingham. It was only when the favourite's support was forfeited that this pack of thwarted courtiers and embittered company directors was loosed upon him and he was ruined.

THE END OF THE REIGN

To Buckingham and Charles, who had assiduously courted both Houses, the results of the 1624 parliament were gratifying. From a more objective standpoint, the powers of the Commons had again been enhanced by court intrigue. A precedent for parliamentary discussion of foreign policy had been created, while the use of impeachment, which enabled parliament to attack ministers without engaging in arguments about prerogative, was an even more sinister development. The government's comprehensive plan for the recovery of the Palatinate proved ruinously expensive, and by August 1624 the Treasurers-at-war reported that nearly £250,000 of the money granted by parliament had been spent. On 4 June a treaty was concluded with the States-General, already at war with Spain, and four regiments of troops were sent to serve under Dutch command. At the same time diplomatic overtures were made to Savoy, Venice and France. The French had recently decided to expel the Spanish from the Valtelline, a strategically valuable area extending northward from Lake Como, which had been occupied by Spanish troops in 1620. A plan was devised for Count Ernest von Mansfeld, a brutal and unprincipled mercenary, to regain both the Palatinate and the Valtelline, and James agreed to supply 13,000 troops to this end, if France would do the same. Mansfeld's expedition was a disaster. The French, having successfully solved the Valtelline problem on their own, refused to allow Mansfeld to disembark his men at Calais and march through France to the Rhine. Shipped instead to Flushing, most of the vagrants who had been conscripted for this army, died of plague and hardship before they had a chance even to engage the enemy.

During negotiations with France, which proceeded throughout the spring, summer and autumn of 1624, James agreed to a marriage between Charles and Henrietta Maria, on the understanding that he must honour his pledge to parliament that no future marriage treaty would grant concessions to English Catholics. When, in August, Richelieu insisted that the treaty should extend to Catholics the privileges so recently offered in Madrid, James terminated negotiations. But the Duke of Buckingham, who was totally committed to a French alliance, joined with Charles to urge James to agree to the French terms. After three days of argument the king gave in, accepting the formula of a secret letter guaranteeing freedom of worship to the Catholics. Buckingham's foreign policy ruined all prospect of continued cooperation between Crown and Commons. The session scheduled for November was postponed until 1625 in the certain knowledge that details of the secret articles would leak out and infuriate parliament. By 1625 the alliance between court faction and parliamentary opposition was in shreds, and by 1626 the duke faced the possibility of impeachment.

The 1624 parliament was prorogued on 29 May and dissolved by the king's sudden death on 27 March 1625. Throughout his life, but particularly during 1624, James had suffered painful and disabling attacks of porphyria **(103)**. In March 1625, resting quietly at Theobalds, he developed a fever and died. His funeral, like his reign, was disorderly and extravagant. The burial took place on 5 May at Westminster Abbey. 'The greatest indeed', wrote Chamberlain, 'that ever was known in England. All was performed with great magnificence but the order was very confused and disorderly. The whole charge is said to have arisen to about £50,000' **(3**, ii, 616).

PART THREE

Assessment

9 Conclusion

'King James slobbered at the mouth and had favourites; he was, thus, a Bad King.' This famous phrase from *1066 And All That* reflects a tradition of writing about James, still common among sixth-formers if not undergraduates, that can be traced to the memoirs of Sir Anthony Weldon, whose congenital malignity and failure to win preferment led him to write his memorable lampoon of the king (23). When, in the nineteenth century, Sir Walter Scott published a *Secret History* of the reign (21), he reprinted the salacious backstairs gossip of Weldon, Arthur Wilson (24), and Thomas Scott (19, 20), and ignored the more sober contemporary histories of William Sanderson (18), and Godfrey Goodman (7), both of whom had written in refutation of such slanders. The first of the Stuarts received little help from the royalists, for men like Sir John Oglander and the Earl of Clarendon sought to excuse the blunders of Charles I by throwing the blame for his troubles on his father (16, 4). The picture of James as a slobbering, cowardly, tactless Scot and a Bad King was planted even more firmly in the popular mind by Scott's novel *The Fortunes of Nigel*, which enjoyed immense popularity at the end of the nineteenth century (62).

More pervasive than the influence of anti-Stuart writers like Weldon has been the work of the great nineteenth-century historian, Samuel Rawson Gardiner, whose *History of England* is a monument of magnificent and careful scholarship, the result of years of pioneering work in the British Museum and Public Record Office, and among Spanish, French and Italian archives (36). It is sometimes observed that Gardiner's background predisposed him to sympathise with the anti-Stuart cause and with nonconformity. His paternal grandmother was descended from Bridget, the eldest daughter of Oliver Cromwell, who married Henry Ireton; and Gardiner's first wife was the youngest daughter of the eccentric nonconformist Edward Irving, in whose church Gardiner served as a deacon from 1851 to 1866. Although Gardiner tried hard to reach balanced judgments and to rid himself of prejudice, his account of James's reign is influenced by a number of questionable preconceptions. He assumes that parliamentary government was the natural and desirable end of constitutional development;

that the House of Commons was invariably right and the king wrong; that 'the root of the old constitution was the responsibility of the Crown to the nation' and that the Stuarts threatened traditional liberties by deliberately violating this constitution. He is not really prepared to examine the case for the king because he does not think there is one; thus he concludes that it was James who 'sowed the seeds of revolution and disaster' (**36**, v, 316).

Twentieth-century historians have presented James in a different perspective, giving proper emphasis to organic weaknesses in the system of government. An archaic financial system that left the Crown dangerously dependent on the goodwill of an increasingly obstreperous Commons made it more than usually difficult to rule England. Fundamental economic problems such as inflation, the collapse of the Old Draperies, the changing structure of foreign trade, the rivalries between trading companies and between London and the outports, and the complex economic fluctuations that caused the Depression of the early 1620s would have puzzled any seventeenth-century government, however competent. Although in many textbooks, Gardiner's influence is still strong, there is now a willingness to understand rather than condemn the king's resistance to parliament's infringements of his hereditary rights. Even his tactlessness can be presented as necessary plain-speaking, for it is clear that the Crown's case was in danger of being lost by default. The Commons and not the king were the innovators, though they were not, of course, consciously seeking sovereign power. Their claim to freedom of speech challenged the way in which the monarch had hitherto exercised his powers, as did their claim in 1605-06 that King and Convocation could not legislate in ecclesiastical affairs. Yet although he felt himself under attack, the king retained a strong sense of the limits of his prerogative in so far as the property of his subjects was concerned, and went out of his way to reassure those who feared the growth of absolutism. James, then, did not set out to destroy the liberties of the subject. Although a great deal of evidence supports the traditional emphasis on conflict between Crown and Commons, the large volume of routine legislation which two out of four of the Jacobean parliaments produced is a measure of the agreement and harmony regularly achieved.

Defenders of King James are fond of saying that if he had died at some time between 1613 and 1616 his reputation would be much higher. This special pleading is considered necessary because the failures of his last years rob him of credit for earlier achievements. The king's handling of the Palatinate crisis, his decline into senility, and his timorous dependence on the Duke of Buckingham are crucial to this interpretation. A king whose guiding principle had been concern for the prerogative and who had opposed the Protestation in 1621 would hardly surrender to the agitation for war against Spain and invite parliament to discuss foreign affairs and the Prince's marriage unless he already had one foot in the grave. This point of view has recently taken some hard knocks, particularly from American historians. There is no doubt that James suffered a serious deterioration of health during the last few years of his life. Chamberlain noticed 'that vigour begins to relent and he must daily more and more intend his own health and quiet'; when too ill to hunt James would settle indoors and have 'his deer brought to make a muster before him'. Yet although some observers certainly emphasised the king's feebleness of mind and body [doc. 13], other evidence suggests that he still kept a firm grip on the formulation of policy. James's handling of foreign affairs between 1618 and 1622 has much to recommend it; he preserved peace while doing as much for Frederick as England's limited resources (and the Palatine himself) would allow. By allowing Charles and Buckingham to visit Madrid the king lost control of the situation and his ambition to preserve peace in his time was shattered. Dr Ruigh's study of the 1624 parliament, however, has demonstrated that any attempt to present James as a geriatric during the last year of his life cannot be reconciled with the evidence (61). By a series of speeches as lucid as any he made ten years earlier, the king insisted that the recovery of the Palatinate and not war against Spain was his government's aim. He successfully prevented the outbreak of open war and managed to direct such military measures as were taken towards Germany, rather than at Spain.

Perhaps the most serious criticism that can be levelled against James I is that his rule opened up an ominous split within the political nation between Court and Country. The administrative preoccupation of much recent research on the early Stuarts has tended to show that it was the politics and personalities of the court, and not a struggle over constitutional and religious principles, that determined the course of events. The king's extravagance and generosity to his courtiers, the sale of titles and offices, the failure to curb administrative costs and corruption, alienated a significant proportion of the country gentry, encouraging them to follow the lead of men who, while pursuing private interests, could honestly attack the faults and failures of the administration. 'My heart is greater than my rent', murmured James, apologetically. His inability to curb his extravagance or wholeheartedly to support reforms which would have cut expenditure, controlled the pension list, established regular accounting in the Exchequer and put an end to the practice of anticipating revenue, was undeniably his greatest fault. As for the king's best-known weakness, some observers drew the worst conclusions. Sir John Oglander remarked that James 'loved young men, his favourites, better than women, loving them beyond the love of men to women. I never saw any fond husband make so great dalliance over his beautiful spouse as I have seen King James over his favourites.' Before convicting James of any perversion other than excessive sentimentality and an emotional dependence on young men, it is worth recalling that the king himself listed sodomy with witchcraft, murder, incest, poisoning and bearing false witness, as 'horrible crimes that ye are bound in conscience never to forgive'. And it does seem odd that the priggish Prince Charles was so friendly with Buckingham if the duke really was his father's lover. Queen Elizabeth, of course, had surrounded herself with handsome young men, but she had never, except momentarily in the case of Essex, allowed them to interfere with her political judgment. James was not so careful. Esmé Stuart, James Hay and Robert Carr were not given much influence, but at the end of his life the king let his policies be swayed by his affection for Buckingham. Professor Zagorin has described how Buckingham's ascendancy 'sowed disaffection in the Court and was the prime cause of enmity on the political scene' (78, p. 59). The patronage system was seriously malformed, causing tremendous resentment among all those who failed to win or buy the Duke's favour. Instead of being used to reward royal service and strengthen the ablest Crown servants, patronage was being used to line the pockets of the Villiers tribe. The Council became less effective in giving advice and pushing through reforms, simply because the majority were Buckingham's creatures. Although the Duke supported Cranfield's economy campaign in the various government departments, he did not allow any interference with the takings of either himself or his family. When the Treasurer opposed the favourite on a matter of policy, even this qualified support was withdrawn and Cranfield fell.

The favourites also caused difficulties by encouraging James to overspend. As Sir Francis Osborne said, with pardonable exaggeration, 'the setting up of these golden calves cost England more than Queen Elizabeth spent in all her wars'. The conspicuous consumption of the Jacobean court generated disapproval among the backwoods gentry. The court had effectively to display the king's majesty and, like any Renaissance court, was bound to be costly. Criticism was inevitable and, in view of James's generosity, extravagance and luxurious tastes, justifiable. It is unjust to blame James because England was, as the Spanish ambassador observed, a land where everyone had his price. Yet the king's cynical tolerance probably made things worse. 'If', said James to the Venetian ambassador, 'I were to imitate the conduct of your republic and begin to punish those who take bribes, I should soon not have a single subject left.' Another cause of the court's unpopularity was the way in which money was raised by the sale of titles, a practice which eroded the hierarchical structure of society and offended the social conventions of the day. Although it was said that the sale of honours defiled the flower of the nobility, at the time it seemed a small price to pay. The practice was widely satirized and the antics of those who bought and sold titles contributed powerfully to the hostility with which the country gentry regarded the court (**65**).

Sensational scandals further damaged the court's reputation. The Essex divorce, the Overbury murder and Suffolk's trial for embezzlement competed for attention with Lady Roos's allegations that her husband was impotent and that the Countess of Exeter was guilty of 'adultery, incest, murder, poison and such-like peccadillos'. Lady Roos was shown to be lying and was herself found guilty of incest with her brother. The Puritan diarist Simonds D'Ewes condemned 'great personages prostituting their bodies to the intent to satisfy and consume their substance in lascivious appetites of all sorts'; his reaction was typical of most of the gentry who saw the court from a distance and disliked what they saw. The 'tone' of the court had important political repercussions, particularly in parliament. It is easy to picture Jacobean courtiers slithering in slime under an easygoing monarch. The courtiers themselves are on record for their criticisms. 'Say to the court it glows and shines like rotten wood,' cried Sir Walter Raleigh. Before being executed for her part in the Overbury murder, the poisoner Mrs Turner lamented: 'O the court! O the court! God bless the King and send him better servants about him, for there is no religion in most of them but malice, pride, whoredom, swearing and rejoicing in the fall of others. It is so wicked a place as I wonder the earth did not open and swallow it up.' In the face of such fervant denunciations it is difficult to keep a sense of proportion. The Elizabethan court, compared with Henry VIII's, was a decorous, family affair where the ruler, because of her sex, took infinite care to avoid scandal. To some extent the 'decadence' of James's court represented a return to normality. James was, however, rather slack about standards of behaviour and morality, and in consequence there was a perceptible falling off in standards as his reign progressed.

Although it would be a mistake to make too much of the words 'Court' and 'Country', which were bandied about as rather casual labels in English politics for many years after 1620, by the end of James's reign these two groups are easily identified. One clustered round the king and the other followed the 'patriots' in the Commons and was characterised by a hearty dislike of all things connected with the court. As Professor Zagorin has put it, 'the term "Country" suggested that the men whom it designated should be regarded as persons of public spirit, unmoved by private interest, untainted by court influence and corruption, representing the highest good of their local communities and the nation in whose interests they, and only they, acted' (78, p. 37).

The king's failings and idiosyncrasies — his vanity and self-importance, his neglect of business in favour of the hunt, his pursuit of witches and pipesmokers, and his desire to be schoolmaster of the realm — should not be allowed to obscure either his virtues or the successes he achieved. James I was shrewd, clever, tolerant and kind, merciful as well as just. There were many during his lifetime who, though critical, appreciated his qualities. In 1619, when the king had just recovered from a serious illness, John Chamberlain wrote: 'I am glad to see the world so tenderly affected toward him, for I assure you all men apprehend what a loss we should have if God should take him from us.' As a politician the king was practical and perceptive, careful not to push his prerogative too far. Despite manifest weaknesses, he did not provoke a major calamity in either of his kingdoms. He made peace with Spain and his mediation abroad helped secure the Truce of Antwerp in 1609 and the Settlement of the Cleves-Jülich dispute in 1612. Ireland was pacified and, for the first time, royal authority established there as effectively as on the border between England and Scotland. During and after the parliament of 1621 an effort was made to make the administration more responsive to trading interests and other opinions. The Privy Council and its *ad hoc* committees attempted to improve the balance of trade by banning the export of bullion, tried hard to alleviate the depression and to deal with the effects of bad harvests.

These efforts were less successful than the king's care of the Church. He put an end to lay exploitation of ecclesiastical property and brought a measure of order and quietness to the Church unknown since before the Reformation. By reasoned discussion and minor compromises, and by distinguishing between godly and subversive Puritans, he won over the majority of nonconformists. His episcopal appointments reflect this emphasis on moderation. Although his bishops, then and now, might not arouse much enthusiasm, neither did they arouse intense hatred. The king also protected the Church courts in a battle with the common lawyers over writs of Prohibition, which halted cases in the ecclesiastical courts until the judges had decided that the case concerned a matter of spiritual and not temporal jurisdiction (12). The common lawyers also disputed the power of High Commission to fine and imprison, powers granted by letters patent and not Act of Parliament. The Commons joined in this attack, directing its fire against the notorious *ex officio* oath. After consulting with the bishops, judges and the Council, James promised minor reforms, and in 1611 issued new letters patent which defined the crimes which came within the Commission's jurisdiction and gave it power to imprison and use the *ex officio* oath (70). In the 1630s Englishmen would look back on James's reign as a golden age of the English Church, during which time a sublime vernacular Bible had been produced, learning and godliness flourished and preachers as diverse as Andrewes, Preston and Donne received royal encouragement. There were no harsh controversies over ceremonies and Church government. Criticisms, of course, there were, but these are best seen as signs of vigour, not chronic discontent.

So instead of approaching the reign with the idea that James I was a Bad King, it is more fruitful to see him as an exceptional man whose qualities fell sadly short of their highest achievement. The judgment of historians is still predominantly unfavourable, as probably it ought to be. Yet because we are more appreciative than nineteenth-century writers of a ruler who brings his people peace, we can give qualified approval to the verdict of Godfrey Goodman, the first of James's defenders, when he wrote:

> Truly all other princes sought unto us and desired the help of King James. He was the occasion of much peace in the Christian world, and certainly held very good correspondence with all the princes of Christendom. . . . While all the Christian world was in wars, he alone governed his people in peace. He was a most just and good king (7, i, 249-50).

PART FOUR

Documents

King James VI, aged 18

M. de Fontenay, Envoy of Mary Stuart, sent this report on the young King to Mary's Secretary, 15 August 1584.

Three qualities of the mind he possesses in perfection: he understands clearly, judges wisely, and has a retentive memory. His questions are keen and penetrating and his replies are sound. In any argument, whatever it is about, he maintains the view that appears to him most just, and I have heard him support Catholic against Protestant opinions. He is well instructed in languages, science, and affairs of State, better, I dare say, than anyone else in his kingdom. In short, he has a remarkable intelligence, as well as lofty and virtuous ideals and a high opinion of himself. . . . He dislikes dancing and music, and the little affectations of courtly life such as amorous discourse or curiosities of dress, and has a special aversion for ear-rings. In speaking and eating, in his dress and in his sports, in his conversation in the presence of women, his manners are crude and uncivil and display a lack of proper instruction. He is never still in one place but walks constantly up and down, though his gait is erratic and wandering, and he tramps about even in his own chamber. His voice is loud and his words grave and sententious. He loves the chase above all other pleasures and will hunt for six hours without inter-ruption, galloping over hill and dale with loosened bridle. His body is feeble and yet he is not delicate. In a word, he is an old young man.

I have remarked in him three defects that may prove injurious to his estate and government: he does not estimate correctly his poverty and insignificance but is over-confident of his strength and scornful of other princes; his love for favourites is indiscreet and wilful and takes no account of the wishes of his people; he is too lazy and indifferent about affairs, too given to pleasure, allowing all business to be conducted by others. Such things are excusable at his age, yet I fear they may become habitual.

Quoted by D. H. Willson, (**75**), p. 53.

Sir Anthony Weldon's character of King James

Weldon (d. 1648) sided with Parliament during the Civil War, during which time he was one of the most virulent critics of the Stuarts. He penned this sketch of James after losing his job as Clerk of the Green Cloth for having written a satire on the Scots, the manuscript of which was found wrapped in one of the records of his department. Of Scotland, he had written: 'The air might be wholesome, but for the stinking people that inhabit it. The ground might be fruitful had they wit to manure it.' And of the Scots: 'To be chained in marriage with one of them, were to be tied to a dead carcase, and cast into a stinking ditch.'

He was of a middle stature, more corpulent through his clothes than in his body, yet fat enough, his clothes ever being made large and easy, the doublets quilted for stiletto proof, his breeches in great pleats and full stuffed. He was naturally of a timorous disposition, which was the reason of his quilted doublets: his eyes large, ever rolling after any stranger that came into his presence, insomuch as many for shame have left the room, as being out of countenance; his beard was very thin: his tongue too large for his mouth, which ever made him speak full in the mouth, and made him drink very uncomely, as if eating his drink, which came out into the cup of each side of his mouth; his skin was as soft as taffeta sarsnet, which felt so, because he never washed his hands, only rubbed his fingers ends slightly with the wet end of a napkin. His legs were very weak, having had (as was thought) some foul play in his youth, or rather before he was born, that he was not able to stand at seven years of age, that weakness made him ever leaning on other men's shoulders; his walk was ever circular, his fingers ever in that walk fiddling about his cod-piece.

He was very temperate in his exercises and in his diet, and not intemperate in his drinking; however, in his old age, [at] Buckingham's jovial suppers, when he had any turn to do with him, made him sometimes overtaken, which he would the very next day remember and repent with tears; it is true he drank very often, which was rather out of a custom than any delight, and his drinks were of the kind for strength, as Frontinack, Canary, High Country wine, Tent Wine and

Scottish Ale, that, had he not had a very strong brain, might have daily been overtaken, although he seldom drank at any one time above four spoonfuls, many times not above one or two.

He was very constant in all things (his favourites excepted), in which he loved change, yet never cast down any (he once raised) from the height of greatness, though from their wonted nearness and privacy, unless by their own default. . . . In his diet, apparel and journeys, he was very constant . . . that the best observing courtier of our time was wont to say, were he asleep seven years, and then awakened, he would tell where the King every day had been, and every dish he had had at table.

He was not very uxorious, though he had a very brave queen that never crossed his designs, nor intermeddled with State affairs, but ever complied with him . . . in the change of favourites; for he was ever best when furthest from his queen, and that was thought to be the first grounds of his often removes, which afterwards proved habitual . . .; he naturally loved not the sight of a soldier, nor of any valiant man. . . .

He was very witty, and had as many ready witty jests as any man living, at which he would not smile himself, but deliver them in a grave and serious manner. He was very liberal of what he had not in his own grip, and would rather part with 100 *li.* he never had in his keeping than one twenty shilling piece within his own custody; he spent much, and had much use of his subjects' purses, which bred some clashings with them in parliament, yet would always come off, and end with a sweet and plausible close. And truly his bounty was not discommendable, for his raising favourites was the worst. Rewarding old servants, and relieving his native countrymen, was infinitely more to be commended in him than condemned. His sending ambassadors were no less chargeable than dishonourable and unprofitable to him and his whole kingdom; for he was ever abused in all negotiations, yet he had rather spend 100,000 *li.* on embassies, to keep or procure peace with dishonour, than 10,000 *li.* on an army that would have forced peace with honour. He loved good laws, and had many made in his time. . . .

. . . He was very crafty and cunning in petty things, as the circumventing any great man, the change of a favourite etc., insomuch as a very wise man was wont to say he believed him the wisest fool in Christendom, meaning him wise in small things, but a fool in weighty affairs. . . .

. . . He was infinitely inclined to peace, but more out of fear than conscience, and this was the greatest blemish this king had through his reign, otherwise (he) might have been ranked with the very best of our kings.

Anthony Weldon, *Character of King James*, in (21), ii, 1-12. There is a fuller extract in (1), pp. 10-16.

document 3

The learned gather at the King's table

That King's table was a trial of Wits. The reading of some Books before him was very frequent, while he was at his Repast. Otherwise he collected Knowledge by variety of Questions, which he carved out to the capacity of his understanding Writers. Methought his hunting Humour was not off so long as his Courtiers, I mean the Learned, stood about him at his Board. He was ever in chase after some disputable Doubts, which he would wind and turn about with the most stabbing Objections that ever I heard. And was as pleasant and fellow-like in all those Discourses as with his Huntsmen in the Field. They that in many such genial and convivial Conferences were ripe and weighty in their Answers were indubiously designed to some Place of Credit and Profit.

John Hacket (8), p. 38.

document 4

Wasteful luxury at Court

In the meantime, the reason King James was so poorly followed, especially in his journeys, was his partiality used towards the Scots, which hung like horseleeches on him, till they could get no more, falling then off by retiring into their own country, or living at ease, leaving all chargeable attendance to the English. The harvest of the love and honour he reaped being suitable to the ill husbandry he used in the unadvised distribution of his favours: For of a number of empty vessels he filled to complete the measure of our infelicity, few proved of use to him, unless such as, by reason of their vast runnings out, had daily need of a new supply: And amongst these the Earl of Carlisle [James Hay] was one of the quorum, that brought in the vanity of ante-suppers, not heard of in our forefathers' time, and, for ought I have read, or, at least remember, unpractised by the most luxurious tyrants. The manner of which was, to have the board covered, at the first entrance of the guests, with dishes, as high as a tall man could well reach, filled with the choicest and dearest viands sea or land could afford: And all this once seen, and having feasted the eyes of the invited, was in a manner thrown away, and fresh set on to the same height, having only this advantage of the other, that it was hot. I cannot forget one of the attendants of the king, that at a feast, made by this monster in excess, eat to his single share a whole pie, reckoned to my lord at ten pounds, being composed of amber-grease, magisteriall of perle, musk, etc. Yet was so far (as he told me) from being sweet in the morning, that he almost poisoned his whole family, flying himself like the satyr from his own stink. And after such suppers huge banquets no less profuse, a waiter returning his servant home with a cloak-bag full of dried sweet-meats and confects, valued to his lordship at more than ten shillings the pound. I am cloyd with the repetition of this excess, no less than scandalized at the continuance of it. . . .

Francis Osborne, *Traditionall Memoyres on the Raigne of King James the First*, printed in *Secret History* (**21**), i, 270-3.

document 5
An attempt to improve the finances, 1617

In the autumn of 1617 James wrote to the Privy Council urging drastic financial reforms.

. . . Long discourses, and fair Tales will never repair my Estate. . . . Remember that I told you that the shoe must be made for the foot, and let that be the Square of all your proceedings in this Business: Abate Superfluities in all things, and Multitudes of unnecessary Officers, where ever they be placed; But for the Household, Wardrobe and Pensions, cut and carve as many as may agree with the possibility of my

Means. . . . In this I expect no Answer in Word or Writing but only the real performance for a beginning to relieve me out of my Miseries, for now the Ball is at your feet, and the world shall bear me Witness, that I have put you fairly to it And so praying God to bless your Labours, I bid you heartily farewell.

Your own James R.

Quoted in (36), iii, 198.

James I on monarchy

In this important speech which James delivered to Parliament on 2. March 1610, he made clear his intention to respect the rights of hi subjects and rule according to the law.

The state of monarchy is the supremest thing upon earth; fo kings are not only God's lieutenants upon earth, and sit upon God's throne, but even by God himself they are called gods There be three principal similitudes that illustrate the state o monarchy: one taken out of the word of God, and the two other out of the grounds of policy and philosophy. In the Scriptures kings are called gods, and so their powers after a certain relation compared to the divine power. Kings are also compared to fathers of families, for the king is truly *paren. patriae*, the politic father of his people. And lastly, kings are compared to the head of this microcosm of the body of man

Kings are justly called gods for that they exercise a manne or resemblance of divine power upon earth, for if you wil consider the attributes to God you shall see how they agree in the person of a king. God hath power to create or destroy make or unmake, at his pleasure; to give life or send death, to judge all and to be judged not accountable to none; to raise low things and to make high things low at his pleasure; and to God are both soul and body due. And the like power have kings: they make and unmake their subjects; they have powe of raising, and casting down; of life, and of death, judges ove all their subjects, and in all causes, and yet accountable to none but God only. They have power to exalt low things, and abase high things, and make of their subjects like men at the chess — a pawn to take a bishop. or a knight — and cry up o

116

down any of their subjects, as they do their money. And to the king is due both the affection of the soul and the service of the body of his subjects. . . .

But yet is all this power ordained by God, *ad aedificationem, non ad destructionem.* For although God hath power as well of destruction, as of creation or maintenance, yet will it not agree with the wisdom of God to exercise his power in the destruction of nature, and overturning the whole frame of things, since his creatures were made, that his glory might thereby be the better expressed. So were he a foolish father that would disinherit or destroy his children without a cause, or leave off the careful education of them; and it were an idle head that would in place of physic so poison or phlebotomise the body as might breed a dangerous distemper or destruction thereof.

But now in these our times we are to distinguish between the state of kings in their first original, and between the state of settled kings and monarchies that do at this time govern in civil kingdoms; for even as God, during the time of the Old Testament, spake by oracles and wrought by miracles, yet how soon it pleased him to settle a Church, which was bought and redeemed by the blood of his only son Christ, then was there a cessation of both, he ever after governing his people and Church within the limits of his revealed will; so in the first original of kings, whereof some had their beginning by conquest, and some by election of the people, their wills at that time served for law, yet how soon kingdoms began to be settled in civility and policy, then did kings set down their minds by laws, which are properly made by the king only, but at the rogation of the people, the king's grant being obtained thereunto. And so the king became to be *lex loquens*, after a sort, binding himself by a double oath to the observation of the fundamental laws of the kingdom: tacitly, as by being a king, and so bound to protect as well the people as the laws of his kingdom; and expressly, by his oath at his coronation. So, as every just king in a settled kingdom is bound to observe that paction made to his people by his laws, in framing his government agreeable thereto, according to that paction which God made with Noah after the deluge, 'Hereafter seed time and harvest, cold and heat, summer and winter, and day and night shall not cease, so long as the earth remains'; and therefore a king governing in a settled kingdom leaves to be a king, and degenerates into a tyrant, as soon as he leaves off to rule according to his laws. . . . As for my part, I thank God I have ever given good proof that I never had intention to the contrary, and I am sure to go to my grave with that reputation and comfort, that never king was in all his time more careful to have his laws duly observed, and himself to govern thereafter, than I.

I conclude then this point touching the power of kings with this axiom of Divinity, that as to dispute what God may do is blasphemy, but *quid vult Deus*, that divines may lawfully and do ordinarily dispute and discuss, for to dispute *a posse ad esse* is both against logic and divinity; so is it sedition in subjects to dispute what a king may do in the height of his power, but just kings will ever be willing to declare what they will do, if they will not incur the curse of God. I will not be content that my power be disputed upon, but I shall ever be willing to make the reason appear of all my doings, and rule my actions according to my laws.

James I, (**10**), pp. 529-31.

document 7

The imprisonment of Sir Thomas Overbury

In 1613 Sir Thomas Overbury was committed to the Tower, for refusing a diplomatic appointment abroad. Contemporaries assumed that this was done to free Robert Carr, Viscount Rochester, from Overbury's influence. In this letter, John Chamberlain tells his friend Sir Dudley Carleton, English ambassador at Venice, what has happened.

I doubt not but you have heard of Sir Thomas Overbury's committing to the Tower the last week. The King hath long had a desire to remove him from about the Lord of Rochester, as thinking it a dishonour to him that the world should have an opinion that Rochester ruled him and Overbury ruled Rochester, whereas he would make it appear that neither Overbury nor Rochester had such a stroke with him, but that he would do what he thought fit and what he intended without acquainting either of them with his purposes and so caused the Lord Chancellor and the Earl of Pembroke to deal with Overbury and to tell him the King's good meaning towards him, whereby he had an intent to make use of his good parts, and to train him for his further service and therefore they offered him his choice to be employed either by the archduke, or into France or into Moscovie, (upon which place we have now new projects). He excused himself as incapable of such places for divers wants and specially of language. They answered that he was young enough and with little labour might attain that in short time, or otherwise he might be assisted and supplied by sufficient secretaries and other fit persons about him: then he alleged indisposition of body and want of health as being much subject to the spleen, whereto they replied that change of air might be a special remedy for such infirmities, but he stood stiffly upon it that he was not willing to forsake his country, and at last gave them a peremptory answer that he could not yield to go, and that he hoped that the King neither in law nor justice could compel him to leave his country, with which answer the King was so incensed, that he willed the Council to consider what it deserved, who upon this contempt caused him to be sent to the Tower. Some take this as a diminution of my Lord of Rochester's credit and favour, but the King told the Council the next day that he would not have it so construed, for that he had, and still did take more delight in his company and conversation than in any man's living.

John Chamberlain, (3), i, 443-4.

document 8

The fall of Somerset: Weldon's account

The revelation, made in 1615, that Sir Thomas Overbury had been murdered while locked in the Tower, caused James considerable embarrassment, and led to the ruin of the Earl of Somerset. Sir Anthony Weldon's account clearly owes much to his imagination and should be compared with that of Godfrey Goodman.

The king with this took his farewell for a time of London, and was accompanied with Somerset to Royston, where no sooner he brought him, but instantly took his leave, little imagining what viper lay among the herbs. Nor must I forget to let you know how perfect the king was in the art of dissimulation, or, to give it his own phrase, king-craft. The Earl of Somerset never parted from him with more seeming affection than at this time, when he knew Somerset should never see him more; and had you seen that seeming affection, (as the author himself did,) you would rather have believed he was in his rising than setting. The earl, when he kissed his hand, the king hung about his neck, slabbering his cheeks, saying, 'For God's sake, when shall I see thee again? On my soul, I shall neither eat nor sleep until you come again.' The earl told him on Monday, (this being on the Friday,) 'For God's sake, let me,' said the king — 'Shall I, shall I?' then lolled about his neck. 'Then, for God's sake, give thy lady this kiss for me.' In the same moment at the stairs head, at the middle of the stairs, and at the stairs foot. The earl was not in his coach when the king used these very words, (in the hearing of four servants, of whom one was Somerset's great creature, and of the Bed-Chamber, who reported it instantly to the author of this history,) 'I shall never see his face more.'

Anthony Weldon, (21), i, 410-12.

document 9

The fall of Somerset: Goodman's account

The true fall of Somerset was this, — that love and affection though they are the strongest passions for the instant, yet they are not of longest continuance, for they are not grounded in judgment, but are rather fancies which follow the eye; and as beauty itself doth decay, so love and affection abate. Take the wisest man; he loves his own children better when they are young than when they are old: so in the best things there is a glut, a surfeit, and a satiety; men are as mean of their pleasures as they are of their labours, and the chief delight which man hath is in change and variety. A man may be glutted with one favourite, as he is feeding upon one food, though it be manna; therefore to have choice of dishes best pleaseth the palate: so truly I think the King was weary of an old favourite.

Now Sir George Villiers had kept much company with the gentlemen waiters, who sometimes after supper did leap and exercise their bodies. But Buckingham of all others was most active; he had a very lovely complexion; he was the handsomest bodied man of England; his limbs so well compacted, and his conversation so pleasing, and of so sweet a disposition. And truly his intellectuals were very great; he had a sound judgment and was of a quick apprehension. . . .

Godfrey Goodman, (7), i, 224-6.

document 10

The king refuses to raise money from the Church, 1621

At this time the king's exchequer grew very low, though Lionel Cranfield, lord treasurer and earl of Middlesex, neglected no means for the improving thereof. In order whereunto, (reader, let this story pass into thy belief on my credit, knowing myself sufficiently assured thereof,) a projector (such necessary evils then much countenanced) informed his majesty of a way whereby speedily to advance much treasure. And how forsooth was it? Even that a new valuation should be made of all spiritual preferments, (which now in the king's books passed at underrates,) to bring them up to or near the full value thereof: this would promote both the casual fines (as I may term them) of first-fruits and the annual rent of tenths to the great advantage of the crown. The king sent to the lord treasurer demanding his judgment thereof.

The treasurer returned his majesty an answer to this effect, so near as I can remember from the mouth of a noble person then present: 'Sir, you have ever been beheld as a great lover and advancer of learned men, and you know clergymen's education is chargeable to them, or their friends; long it is before they get any preferment, which at last generally is but small in proportion to their pains and expenses. Let it not be said that you gained by grinding them; other ways less obnoxious to just censure will be found out to furnish your occasions.' The king commended Cranfield, (as doing it only for trial,) adding moreover, 'I should have accounted thee a very knave if encouraging me herein'; and so the project was blasted for the present, as it was when it budded again, propounded by some unworthy instrument, in the reign of King Charles.

Thomas Fuller, (6), v, 489-90.

The Commons' declaration, 4 June 1621

At the close of the first session of the 1621 parliament Sir John Perrot gravely directed the attention of the Commons to the dangers threatening Protestantism at home and abroad. He proposed that if the Palatinate could not be regained by negotiation, they should undertake to risk their lives and estates for the defence of Frederick. Perrot's motion was carried by acclamation and was transposed into the more formal language of a Declaration, which the king had translated into the main European languages for circulation abroad. It is not, therefore, surprising that the king expected a quick and generous supply when parliament met again in November.

The Commons asembled in Parliament, taking into consideration the present estate of the King's children abroad, and the general afflicted estate of the professors of the same Christian religion professed by the Church of England and other foreign parts; and being troubled with a true sense and fellow-feeling of their distresses as members of the same body, do, with one unanimous consent of themselves and of the whole body of the kingdom whom they do represent, declare unto the whole world their hearty grief and sorrow for the same; and do not only join with them in their humble and devout prayers to Almighty God to protect his true church, and to avert the dangers now threatened, but also with one heart and voice do solemnly protest that, if his Majesty's pious endeavours by treaty to procure their peace and safety shall not take that good effect he desireth, in the treaty whereof they humbly beseech his Majesty to make no long delay; — that then, upon the signification of his pleasure in parliament, they shall be ready, to the uppermost of their powers, both with their lives and fortunes, to assist him; so as, by the Divine help of Almighty God, who is never wanting unto those who, in His fear shall undertake the defence of His own cause, he may be able to do that by his sword which by peaceable courses shall not be effected.

Quoted in **(36)**, iv, 129.

The Commons' protestation, 18 December 1621

In December 1621, James wrote from Newmarket forbidding the Commons to 'meddle with anything concerning our government or deep matters of state', and informing them 'that we think ourself very free and able to punish any man's misdemeanor in Parliament . . .' After explaining their attitude to the king, and having listened to his reply, the Commons decided to enter a statement of their privileges in the Journal of the House.

The Commons now assembled in Parliament, being justly occasioned thereunto concerning sundry liberties, franchises and privileges of Parliament, amongst others here mentioned, do make this Protestation following. That the liberties, franchises, privileges and jurisdictions of Parliament are the ancient and undoubted birthright and inheritance of the subjects of England; and that the arduous and urgent affairs concerning the King, state and defence of the realm, and of the Church of England, and the maintenance and making of laws, and redress of mischiefs and grievances which daily happen within this realm, are proper subjects and matters of counsel and debate in Parliament; and that in the handling and proceeding of those businesses every Member of the House of Commons hath, and of right ought to have, freedom of speech to propound, treat, reason and bring to conclusion the same; and that the Commons in Parliament have like liberty and freedom to treat of these matters in such order as in their judgements shall seem fittest; and that every Member of the said House hath like freedom from all impeachment, imprisonment and molestation (other than by censure of the House itself) for or concerning any speaking, reasoning or declaring of any matter or matters touching the Parliament or Parliament business; and that if any of the said members be complained of and questioned for anything done or said in Parliament, the same is to be showed to the King by the advice and assent of all the Commons assembled in Parliament before the King give credence to any private information.

From J. Rushworth, ed. *Historical Collections of Private Passages of State* (8 vols, London, 1659-1701), i, 53. There is a full documentation in (22), pp. 279-288.

The king's poor health and waning influence, 1623

During the years 1621-1623 both the Venetian and French ambassadors commented on the king's declining powers, assuming that his grasp on affairs was slipping at the same time. This letter from Alvise Valaresse, the Venetian Ambassador in England, was written to the Doge and Senate on 20 February 1623.

... I abstained from asking for a special audience but caused my very good friend the lord chamberlain to inform his Majesty that I should like to see him before he left, although I knew the pressure of his affairs, and the weak state of his health, so that I would wait upon his pleasure. The king replied that he appreciated my courtesy, and said he wished to have the purer air of the country for his complete recovery. So he went two days ago to Theobalds with the idea of proceeding to Newmarket later on. It may be that the remains of his last attack of gout have added to his usual aversion for audiences. ... In his Majesty's lethal sickness it would certainly have been desirable, as a symptom and sign of life, if he had recognized his own will in the good resolutions of others. But I must repeat, however sadly, that all good sentiments are clearly dead in the king. He is too blind in disordered self love and his wish for quiet and pleasure, too agitated by constant mistrust of everyone, tyrannized over by perpetual fear for his life, tenacious of his authority as against the parliament and jealous of the prince's obedience, all accidents and causes of his fatal and almost desperate infirmity of mind, so harmful to the general welfare. Nevertheless if the king was ever capable of improvement, or if his actions hitherto were merely dissimulation ... who knows if some unexpected but very necessary change might not come over the king. But though possible this is very unlikely, but as impossible things are sometimes taken into consideration by prudent men, it is easy to recognize the consequences, if such a change ever took place, of contemptuously refraining from telling him of a thing, not indeed accomplished but published everywhere.

From *Calendar of State Papers and Manuscripts existing in the Archives of Venice*, 1621-1623, ii, 571-2.

A game at chess

In 1624, in his play 'A Game at Chess', Thomas Middleton presented a thinly disguised Count Gondomar as leader of a pro-Spanish spy ring. In this extract the Black Knight (Gondomar) recounts his achievements:

> 'I have sold the groom of the stool six times . . .
> . . . I have taught our friends, too
> To convey White House [English] gold to our
>   Black Kingdom [Spain]
> In cold baked pastries and so cozen searchers . . .
> Letters conveyed in rolls, tobacco-balls . . .
> . . . Pray, what use
> Put I my summer recreation to,
> But more to inform my knowledge in the state
> And strength of the White Kingdom? No fortification
> Haven, creek, landing place about the White Coast,
> But I got draft and platform; learned the depth
> Of all their channels, knowledge of all sands,
> Shelves, rocks and rivers for invasion properest;
> A catalogue of all the navy royal,
> The burden of the ships, the brassy murderers,
> The number of the men, to what cape bound:
> Again for the discovery of the islands,
> Never a shire but the state better known
> To me than to her best inhabitants;
> What power of men and horses, gentry's revenues,
> Who well affected to our side, who ill,
> Who neither well nor ill, all the neutrality:
> Thirty-eight thousand souls have been seduced, Pawn,
> Since the jails vomited with the pill I gave 'em.'

(IV, ii, 41-75).

Thomas Middleton, *A Game at Chess*, ed. E. C. Bald, Cambridge University Press, 1929.

Anti-Spanish propaganda, 1624

Middleton's play is a lurid piece of anti-Spanish, anti-Catholic propaganda which was performed by the King's Players at the Globe Playhouse in August 1624. 'A Game at Chess' had been licensed on 12 June, but was not acted until 6 August, by which time King James was out of London. It ran for nine days before the king heard of it, and commanded the Players to cease. The Spanish ambassador had reported the affair to James, before writing this letter to Count Olivares in Madrid.

The actors whom they call here 'the King's Men' have recently acted, and are still acting, in London a play that so many people come to see, that there were more than 3,000 there on the day that the audience was smallest. There was such merriment, hubbub and applause that even if I had been many leagues away it would not have been possible for me not to have taken notice of it. . . . The subject of the play is a game of chess, with white squares and black squares, their kings and other pieces, acted by the players, and the king of the blacks has easily been taken for our lord the King, because of his youth, dress and other details. The first act, or rather game was played by their ministers, impersonated by the white pieces, and the Jesuits, by the black ones. Here there were remarkable acts of sacrilege and, among other abominations, a minister summoned St Ignatius from hell, and when he found himself again in the world, the first thing he did was to rape one of his female penitents; in all this, these accursed and abominable men revealed the depths of their heresy by their lewd and obscene actions. The second act was directed against the Archbishop of Spalatro, at that time a white piece, but afterwards won over to the black side by the Count of Gondomar, who, brought on to the stage in his litter almost to the life, and seated in his chair with a hole in it (they said), confessed all the treacherous actions with which he had deceived and soothed the king of the whites, and, when he discussed the matter of confession with the Jesuits, the actor disguised as the Count took out a book in which were rated all the prices for which henceforwards sins were to be forgiven. . . . The last act ended with a long, obstinate struggle between all the whites and the blacks, and in it he who acted the Prince of Wales heartily beat and kicked the 'Count of Gondomar' into Hell, which consisted of a great hole and hideous figures; and the white king (drove) the black king and even his queen (into Hell) almost as offensively. . . . It cannot be pleaded that those who repeat and hear these insults are merely four rogues because during these last four days more than 12,000 persons have all heard the play of *A Game at Chess*, for so they call it, including all the nobility still in London. All these people come out of the theatre so inflamed against Spain that, as a few Catholics have told me who went secretly to see the play, my person would not be safe in the streets; others have advised me to keep to my house with a good guard, and this is being done.'

Don Carlos Coloma to the Count-Duke of Olivares, 10 August 1624, reproduced in G. E. Bentley, *The Jacobean and Caroline Stage* (Oxford University Press, 1956), iv, 871-2.

document 16

The Spanish Marriage Treaty: the secret clauses, July 1624

After the Spanish Marriage Treaty had been ratified in the Chapel Royal at Whitehall, James withdrew with the Spanish ambassadors to swear to four 'private articles' which were kept secret.

1. That particular Laws made against Roman Catholics, under which other Vassals of our Realms are not comprehended . . . as likewise general Laws under which all are equally comprised, if so be they are such which are repugnant to the Romish religion, shall not at any time hereafter . . . be put in execution against the said Roman Catholics. . . .
2. That no other Laws shall hereafter be made anew against the said Roman Catholics, but that there shall be a perpetual Toleration of the Roman Catholic Religion within private houses throughout all our Realms and Dominions, which we will have to be understood as well of our Kingdoms of *Scotland* and *Ireland* as in *England*. . . .
3. That neither by us, nor by any other interposed person whatsoever, directly or indirectly, privately or publicly, will we treat (or attempt) anything with the most renowned Lady Infanta *Donna Maria*, which shall be repugnant to the Roman Catholic religion; Neither will we by any means persuade her that she should ever renounce or relinquish the same in substance or form. . . .
4. That We and the Prince of *Wales* will interpose our authority, and will do as much as in us shall lie, that the Parliament shall approve, confirm and ratify all and singular Articles in

favour of the Roman Catholics, capitulated between the most renowned Kings by reason of this Marriage; And that the said Parliament shall revoke and abrogate particular laws made against the said Roman Catholics. . . .

From John Rushworth, *Historical Collections*, (London, 1659), p. 86.

Buckingham reproves the king: 3 March 1624

In 1624, while Charles and Buckingham were encouraging the House of Commons to denounce Spain, the king continued to seek a negotiated settlement of the Palatinate question. When he refused to see the duke, closeting himself with the Spanish envoys instead, Buckingham sent this angry letter.

Notwithstanding of this unfavourable interpretation I find made of a thankful and loyal heart in calling my words crude catonic words, in obedience of your commands I will tell the House of Parliament, that you, having been upon the fields this afternoon, have taken such a fierce rheum and cough, as not knowing how you will be this night, you are not yet able to appoint them a day of hearing, but I will forbear to tell them that, notwithstanding of your cold, you were able to speak with the King of Spain's instruments, though not with your own subjects. All I can say is, you march slowly towards your own safety, those that depend of you. I pray God at last you may attain to it, otherwise I shall take little comfort in wife or child, though now I am suspected to look more to the rising sun than my maker. Sir, hitherto I have tied myself to a punctual answer of yours. If I should give myself leave to speak my own thoughts, they are so many that, though the quality of them should not grieve you coming from one you willfully and unjustly deject, yet the number of them are so many that I should not give over till I had troubled you; therefore I will only tie myself to that which shall be my last and speedy refuge, to pray the Almighty to increase your joys and qualify the sorrows of your Majesty's

humble slave and dog,

STEENIE

Quoted in (**61**), p. 190.

Buckingham urges James to make concessions to the Commons, 4 March 1624

These suggestions of the Duke of Buckingham were incorporated in an address to both Houses of Parliament after James had accepted their advice to break off the treaties with Spain. The effect was deadened when the King reiterated his reluctance 'without Necessity, to embroil myself with War'.

That you did not mean to put a scorn upon them, to call for their advice, and then to reject it, if they pay no real assistance with it.

First to give them thanks for their uniform offer of (assistance in their) advice.

Then to take notice of their careful proceedings in the Lower House.

That you do not desire to engage them in their gift till you be declared anent their advice.

And if you be engaged into a war by their advice you mean not to hearken to a peace without first hearing them.

And that they may see your sincere dealing with them you will be contented that they choose a committee to see the issuing out of the money they give for the recovery of the Palatinate in case you accept their advice.

Then to show them that this is the fittest time that ever presented itself to make a right understanding between you and your people, and you assure yourself that their behaviour will so continue as they have begun towards you that they shall see by proofs how far you will be in love with parliaments for making of good laws and reforming of abuses.

Quoted by R. E. Ruigh (**61**), p. 199.

James warns the Commons not to meddle in the prosecution of the war

When, on 23 March 1624, James accepted the Commons' offer of money and promised to dissolve the treaties with Spain, he told them

*that he would never allow any parliamentary interference in the pros-
ecution of the war.*

Yet I desire you to think that I must have a faithful and
secret council of war, and which must not be ordered by a
multitude, for so my designs may be discovered beforehand
and I shall purpose nothing that the enemy will not know as
well as I. Whether, therefore, I shall send 2,000 or 10,000,
whether by sea or by land, north or south, by diversion or
otherwise by invading the Bavarian or the Emperor, that
must be in the council of my own heart, and that you must
leave to the King. But every penny bestowed shall be in the
sight of your own committees; their hands only shall be in
the bag; yet how much shall go out, or how little, must be in
the power of the King, whose war it is, whose stewards they
are.

Robert Horne, *Synopsis of proceedings in the House of Commons*, 23
February to 9 April 1624. Bodleian Library, Tanner MS. 392. Quoted
in **(61)**, p. 231.

Bibliography

What follows is not a full bibliography but a list of books and articles referred to in the text. There is good, short introduction to James's reign in Maurice Ashley, *England in the Seventeenth Century*, 2nd edn, Penguin, 1960. The most recent and possibly the best general survey is Conrad Russell's *The Crisis of Parliaments: English History 1509-1660*, Oxford University Press, 1971. The best biography is D. H. Willson, *James VI & I*, Cape, 1956.

DOCUMENTS AND CONTEMPORARY ACCOUNTS

1   Ashton, R., *James I by his Contemporaries*, Hutchinson, 1969.
2   Birch, Thomas, *Court and Times of James I*, ed. R. F. Williams, 2 vols, London, 1849.
3   Chamberlain, John, *The Letters of John Chamberlain*, ed. N. E. McClure, 2 vols, Philadelphia, 1939.
4   Clarendon, Edward Earl of, *The History of the Rebellion and Civil Wars in England*, ed. W. D. Macray, 2 vols, Oxford, 1888.
5   *Commons Debates 1621*, ed. W. Notestein, F. H. Relf and H. Simpson, 7 vols, New Haven, Yale University Press, 1935.
6   Fuller, Thomas, *The Church History of Britain*, ed. J. S. Brewer, 6 vols, Oxford, 1845.
7   Goodman, Godfrey, *The Court of James I*, ed. J. S. Brewer, 2 vols, London, 1839.
8   Hacket, John, *Scrinia Reserata: A Memorial Offer'd to the Great Deservings of John Williams D.D.*, London, 1692.
9   *Historical Collections*, ed. John Rushworth, London, 1659.
10 James I, *Works*, London, 1616.
11 Jones, W. J., *Politics and the Bench*, Allen & Unwin, 1971.
12 Kenyon, J. P., *The Stuart Constitution*, Cambridge University Press, 1966.
13 *Lords Debates 1624 and 1626*, Notes of the Debates in the House of Lords, Officially taken by Henry Elsing, Clerk of the Parliaments, A.D. 1624 & 1626, ed. S. R. Gardiner, Camden Society, new series, vol 24, London, 1879.

14 McIlwain, C. H., ed., *The Political Works of James I*, New York, Russell, 1965.

15 *Narrative of the Spanish Marriage Treaty*, Francisco de Jesus, ed. and trans. S. R. Gardiner, Camden Society, vol. 101, London, 1869.

16 Oglander, Sir John, *A Royalist's Notebook*, ed. Francis Bamford, London, Constable, 1936.

17 *Proceedings in Parliament, 1610*, ed. E. R. Foster, Yale University Press, 1966.

18 Sanderson, William, *A Compleat History*, London, 1656.

19 Scott, Thomas, *Vox Populi or Newes from Spayne*, York (?), 1620.

20 Scott, Thomas, *The Second Part of Vox Populi*, York, 1624.

21 *Secret History of the Court of James I*, 2 vols, ed. W. Scott, Edinburgh, 1811.

22 Tanner, J. R., *Constitutional Documents of the Reign of James I*, Cambridge University Press, 1930.

23 Weldon, Sir Anthony, *The Court and Character of James I* (1650), reprinted in *Secret History* . . . ed. W. Scott, Edinburgh, 1811.

24 Wilson, Arthur, *The Life and Reign of James the First, King of Great Britain*, London 1653, reprinted in White Kennett, *A Complete History of England with the Lives of all the Kings and Queens Hereof*, vol. 2, pp. 661-792, London, 1719.

25 Wilson, Thomas, *The State of England Anno Dom. 1600*, ed. F. J. Fisher, Camden Miscellany, 1936.

SECONDARY WORKS

26 Ashton, R., *The Crown and the Money Market 1603-1640*, Oxford University Press, 1960.

27 Aston, T., *Crisis in Europe 1560-1660*, Routledge, 1965.

28 Babbage, S. B., *Puritanism and Richard Bancroft*, S.P.C.K., 1962.

29 Barnes, T. G., *Somerset, 1625-1640: A County's Government during the 'Personal Rule'*, Oxford University Press, 1961.

30 Brett-James, N., *The Growth of Stuart London*, Allen & Unwin, 1935.

31 Carter, C. H., *The Secret Diplomacy of the Habsburgs*, Columbia University Press, 1964.

32 Collinson, Patrick, *The Elizabethan Puritan Movement*, Cape, 1967.

33 Dietz, F. C., *English Public Finance 1558-1641*, London, Appleton-Century, 1932.

34 Donaldson, Gordon, *Scotland: James V – James VII*, Edinburgh University Press, 1965.

35 Friis, Astrid, *Alderman Cockayne's Project and the Cloth Trade*, Copenhagen and Oxford, 1927.

36 Gardiner, S. R., *History of England 1603-1642*, first 5 vols, London 1864-86.

37 George, C. H. and George, K., *The Protestant Mind of the English Reformation, 1570-1640*, Princeton University Press, 1961.

38 Haller, W., *The Rise of Puritanism*, New York, 1938.

39 Hembry, P. M., *The Bishops of Bath and Wells 1540-1640*, Athlone Press, 1967.

40 Hill, Christopher, *The Century of Revolution 1603-1714*, Nelson, 1961.

41 Hill, Christopher, *The Economic Problems of the Church from Archbishop Whitgift to the Long Parliament*, Oxford University Press, 1956.

42 Hill, Christopher, *Puritanism and Revolution*, Secker & Warburg, 1958.

43 Hill, Christopher, *Reformation to Industrial Revolution*, Weidenfeld & Nicolson, 1967; rev. edn, Penguin Books, 1969.

44 Hill, Christopher, *Society and Puritanism in Pre-Revolutionary England*, Secker & Warburg, 1964; Panther, 1969.

45 Hurstfield, Joel, *The Queen's Wards*, Longmans, 1958.

46 Judson, M. A., *The Crisis of the Constitution: an Essay in Constitutional and Political Thought in England, 1603-1645*, Rutgers University Press, 1949.

47 Laslett, Peter, *The World We Have Lost*, Methuen, 1965.

48 Lee, Maurice, *James I and Henri IV: An Essay in English Foreign Policy 1603-1610*, University of Illinois Press, 1970.

49 Marchant, R., *The Puritans and the Church Courts in the Diocese of York 1560-1642*, Cambridge University Press, 1960.

50 Mathew, David, *The Jacobean Age*, Longmans, 1941.

51 Mathew, David, *James I*, Eyre & Spottiswoode, 1967.

52 Mattingly, Garrett, *Renaissance Diplomacy*, Cape, 1962.

53 McGrath, P. V., *Papists and Puritans under Elizabeth I*, Blandford, 1967.

54 Mitchell, W. B., *The Rise of the Revolutionary Party in the English House of Commons 1603-1629*, New York, Columbia University Press, 1957.

55 Moir, T. L., *The Addled Parliament of 1614*, Oxford University Press, 1958.

56 Nef, J. U., *Industry and Government in France and England, 1540-1640*, Oxford University Press, 1940.

57 New, J. F. H., *Anglican and Puritan: the basis of their opposition, 1558-1640*, A. and C. Black, 1964.

58 Notestein, Wallace, *The House of Commons 1604-1610*, Yale University Press, 1971.

59 Prestwich, Menna, *Cranfield: Business and Politics under the Early Stuarts*, Oxford University Press, 1966.

60 Reinmuth, H. S., Jr., ed., *Early Stuart Studies*, University of Minnesota Press, 1970.

61 Ruigh, R. E., *The Parliament of 1624*, Oxford University Press, 1971.

62 Scott, Walter, *The Fortunes of Nigel*, 2 vols, London 1879 (vols 26-27, Waverley Novels, illust. edn, 48 vols, London, 1877-9).

63 Seaver, P. S., *The Puritan Lectureships*, Stanford University Press, 1970.

64 Simpson, A., *The Wealth of the Gentry, 1540-1640*, University of Chicago Press, 1961.

65 Stone, Lawrence, *The Crisis of the Aristocracy, 1558-1641*, Oxford University Press, 1965.

66 Stone, Lawrence, ed., *Social Change and Revolution in England 1540-1640*, Longmans, 1965 (a selection of writings and documents relating to the gentry controversy, with an introduction and bibliography).

67 Supple, B. E., *Commercial Crisis and Change in England 1600-1642*, Cambridge University Press, 1959.

68 Tawney, R. H., *Business and Politics under James I*, Cambridge University Press, 1958.

69 Usher, R. G., *The Reconstruction of the English Church*, 2 vols, New York, 1910.

70 Usher, R. G., *The Rise and Fall of High Commission*, Oxford University Press, 1913.

71 Watkin, E. I., *Roman Catholicism in England from the Reformation to 1950*, Oxford University Press, 1957.

72 Welsby, P. A., *George Abbot, The Unwanted Archbishop 1562-1633*, S.P.C.K., 1962.

73 Welsby, P. A., *Lancelot Andrewes, 1555-1625*, S.P.C.K., 1958.

74 Wilson, Charles, *England's Apprenticeship, 1603-1763*, Longmans, 1965.

75 Willson, D. H., *James VI & I*, Cape, 1956.

76 Willson, D. H., *The Privy Councillors in the House of Commons, 1604-1629*, Minneapolis, 1940.

77 Wormuth, F. D., *The Royal Prerogative, 1603-1649*, Ithaca, New York, 1939.

78 Zagorin, Perez, *The Court and the Country: The Beginning of the English Revolution*, Routledge, 1969.

79 Zaller, R. B., *The Parliament of 1621: a Study in Constitutional Conflict*, California University Press, 1971.

ARTICLES AND ESSAYS

The following abbreviations are used:

AmHR	American Historical Review
BIHR	Bulletin of the Institute of Historical Research
CHJ	Cambridge Historical Journal
EcHR	Economic History Review
H	History
HLQ	Huntingdon Library Quarterly
NCMH	New Cambridge Modern History
PP	Past and Present

80 Carter, C. H., 'Gondomar: ambassador to James I, *CHJ* vol. 6, 1964.

81 Coakley, T. M., 'Robert Cecil in power', **(60)**, pp. 64-95.

82 Cooper, J. R., 'Differences between English and Continental governments in the early seventeenth century', in *Britain and the Netherlands*, ed. Bromley, J. S. and Kossmann, E. H., Chatto & Windus, 1960.

83 Cooper, J. R., 'The fall of the Stuart Monarchy', in *NCMH* vol. 4, pp. 531-84, Cambridge University Press, 1970.

84 Curtis, M. H., 'The alienated intellectuals in early Stuart England', *PP* vol. 23, 1962.

85 Curtis, M. H., 'The Hampton Court Conference and its aftermath', *H* vol. 46, 1961.

86 Davies, G., 'The Character of James I', *HLQ* vol. 5, 1942.

87 Elton, G., 'A high road to civil war?' in *From the Renaissance to the Counter-Reformation*, ed. C. H. Carter, New York, 1965.

88 Fisher, F. J., 'London's export trade in the early seventeenth century', *EcHR* vol. 3, 1950-51.

89 Foster, E. R., 'The procedure of the House of Commons against patents and monopolies 1621-4', in *Conflict in Stuart England. Essays in honour of Wallace Notestein*, ed. B. D. Henning, Cape, 1960.

90 George, C. H., 'Puritanism as history and historiography', *PP* vol. 41, 1968.

91 Gould, J. D., 'The trade depression of the early 1620s', *EcHR* vol. 7, 1954-55.

92 Hall, B., 'Puritanism: the problem of definition', in *Studies in Church History,* vol. 2, ed. G. J. Cuming, Ecclesiastical History Society, 1965.

93 Hinton, R. W. K., 'The decline of parliamentary government under Elizabeth I and the early Stuarts', *CHJ* vol. 13, 1957.

94 Hurstfield, J., 'Political corruption in modern England: the historian's problem', *H* vol. 52, 1967.

95 Hurstfield, J., 'The political morality of early Stuart statesmen', *H* vol. 56, 1971.

96 Hurstfield, J., 'Social structure, Office-holding and Politics, Chiefly in Western Europe', in *NCMH* vol. 3, pp. 126-48, Cambridge University Press, 1968.

97 Hurstfield, J., 'The succession struggle in late Elizabethan England', in *Elizabethan Government and Society: essays presented to Sir John Neale,* eds. S. T. Bindoff, J. Hurstfield and C. H. Williams, Athlone Press, 1961.

98 Kautz, A. P., 'The selection of Jacobean bishops', in **(60)**, pp. 152-80.

99 Kennedy, D. E., 'The Jacobean episcopate', *CHJ* vol. 5, 1962.

100 Lee, M., 'The Jacobean diplomatic service', *AmHR* vol. 72, 1967.

101 Loomie, A. J., 'Sir Robert Cecil and the Spanish embassy', *BIHR* vol. 42, 1969.

102 Loomie, A. J., 'Toleration and diplomacy: the religious issue in Anglo-Spanish relations, 1603-1605', *Transactions of the American Philosophical Society,* vol. 53, part 6, Philadelphia, 1963.

103 Macalpine, I., Hunter, R. and Rimington, C., 'Porphyria in the Royal Houses of Stuart, Hanover and Prussia', *British Medical Journal*, vol. 6, Jan. 1968. Reprinted in *Porphyria – a Royal Malady*, British Medical Assoc., 1968.

104 McIlwain, C. H., 'The English Common Law as a barrier against absolutism', *AmHR* vol. 49, 1943.

105 Mousley, J. E., 'The fortunes of some gentry families in Elizabethan Sussex', *EcHR*, 2nd series, vol. 11, 1958-59.

106 Neale, J. R., 'The Elizabethan political scene', in *Essays in Elizabethan History*, Cape, 1958, pp. 59-84.

107 Notestein, Wallace, 'The winning of the initiative by the House of Commons', Raleigh Lecture, 1924.

108 Stone, Lawrence, 'The fruits of office: the case of Robert Cecil, first Earl of Salisbury, 1596-1612', in *Essays in the Economic and Social History of Tudor and Stuart England*, ed. F. J. Fisher, Cambridge University Press, 1961.

109 Stone, Lawrence, 'Social mobility in England, 1500-1700', *PP* vol. 33, 1966.

110 Trevor-Roper, Hugh, 'James I and his Bishops', in *Historical Essays*, Macmillan, 1963, pp. 130-46.

111 Willson, D. H., 'King James I and Anglo-Scottish unity', in *Conflict in Stuart England*, ed. Henning, 1960.

112 Wright, L. B., 'Propaganda against James I's appeasement of Spain', *HLQ* vol. 6, 1942-3.

Index